Peace by Piece:

A Story of Survival and Forgiveness

As told by Peter Loth
Written by Sandra Kellogg Rath

Peace by Piece:
A Story of Survival and Forgiveness
As told by Peter Loth
Written by Sandra Kellogg Rath

Printed in the United States of America

ISBN 978-1-60647-121-0

www.xulonpress.com

To my two mothers: Julianna Szczepańska, the mother who adopted me as her own, sacrificing all she had to keep me safe and out of harm's way; and

Helena Loth, the mother who gave me life, sacrificing her integrity to keep me alive, at the risk of being misunderstood.

To my childhood friend, Gwiazda (Star). Our story has been told. You were my true friend, and I look forward to seeing you in Heaven.

To all the children who suffered and died needlessly — they now know peace.

To my wife, Val; my children: Bridgette, Pete, Jason, Sandy, Natassia, Katerina, Juliana, and Phillip, and all of my grandchildren — present and future; my sisters, Georgia and Barbara; and my cousin, Ulrich — may you never forget our past and always walk in forgiveness. I love you all.

Acknowledgements

Sandy Kellogg Rath, my stepdaughter — This book became a reality because of your compassion, love, and commitment to the truth. You were there with me through all of it — thank you. I love you.

Susan Simon — Thank you for taking my story to your heart and for giving so much time out of your life to edit this book to make it right. You will always be in my heart.

U.S. Representative Ike Skelton, Sheriff Gene Darnell, the Thoman family, the Homfeld family, and Mary Linda Rekhopf — Thank you for accepting me, showing me love, and giving me a fresh start. May God bless you.

The American Red Cross in Lake City, Florida, and Washington, D.C. — Thank you for your research in helping me to find the truth about my life.

Nathan Rath — You were the wind beneath Sandy's wings while she was writing. She couldn't have done it without your love and support. Thank you.

Jason Kellogg and Larry Kellogg — Thank you for all of your sound legal advice. You've always been there for me — it means a lot.

Billy and Kathy Banks — There are no words strong enough to thank you for your friendship.

Larry and Beverly Williams; Gil and Susie Ebarb; Dave and Debbie Bridwell; and Jerry Thomason — Thank you for always encouraging me with your friendship and prayers.

Author's Note

This is a book about suffering, survival, and ultimately forgiveness. Suffering and survival are not always pleasant topics to contemplate or read about, but without them there is no clear understanding of the need for and power of forgiveness. In an effort to accurately depict the — at times horrific — events of Peter's life, there are several very graphic scenes of abuse. Please exercise discretion with younger readers.

Prologue

Summers in Florida are brutal. That was my conclusion as I sat on the roof trying to hook up a satellite dish. If it wasn't the sweat dripping into my eyes, it was the gnats.

My family and I lived in northern Florida, an hour and a half away from both the Atlantic Ocean and the Gulf of Mexico. We had been building our home for several years, but it always needed more money and more work.

My family was pretty good about living in an unfinished home, but the most common complaint was the fact that we only got one television station. I had to agree. Since Juliana and Phillip, my two youngest children, loved watching TV with the family at night, I decided to be a good dad and buy a satellite dish. I thought I would be smart and wait until the sun had begun to set before installing it, but the humidity still managed to get to me.

On top of the heat, the reception wouldn't come in no matter which way I moved the satellite dish. I tried it right side up, upside down, sideways, on one end of the roof and then the other, all to no avail. I just wanted to hook it up, take a shower, and relax on the couch watching a channel other than CBS. That wasn't going to happen anytime soon.

As I stood on the ladder feeling more than frustrated, I heard the telephone ring inside the house. I almost hoped it was for me, so I wouldn't have to deal with the satellite dish.

A few moments passed before the sliding glass door from the kitchen flung open and my wife stood beneath me with concern in her eyes.

"What's wrong, Val?" I asked. She didn't respond. "Val?"

"Uh, I think you better take this call," she said hesitantly.

I scrambled down the ladder, the uneasiness in my wife's voice making my stomach do flips. I was certain someone had been hurt or killed. I wiped the sweat from my forehead, took off my grimy shirt and followed Val into the kitchen.

"You might want to sit down for this," she said as she pulled out a chair for me. I blindly obeyed.

She handed me the phone and took another chair at the kitchen table. I held the phone for a moment and then answered.

"Hello?" I asked with a shaky voice.

"Peter?" a woman's voice at the other end responded.

"Yes."

"Peter Loth?"

"Yes, that's me." I was afraid from the hesitancy in her voice that something had happened to one of my older children.

"Peter, this is your little sister, Barbara."

I nearly dropped the phone.

Tears welled up in my eyes. My wife reached over and patted my arm. I couldn't answer at first. My mind was racing.

Long dormant feelings flooded me. I was reminded of my childhood and all of the pain. I vividly remembered the events that led up to leaving my sisters. I never even had a chance to say goodbye. At the time, I wasn't sure I would ever see or hear from them again.

Those memories continued to haunt me. I wondered: if I had the chance to go back, would I have done things differently? *Could* I have done things differently?

Unfortunately, the painful memories didn't stop with the night I left my sisters. My mother had abandoned me when I was a baby, which in my mind meant that she didn't want me. It was a truth I learned to deal with daily. I suppose one never fully gets over the feeling of abandonment. All the hurt and disappointment from that rejection lingered with me into adulthood as my constant companion.

In moments when I least expected it, the hurt would creep in and the pain would overwhelm me.

For a long time I was able to ignore the wounds. I pretended that my birth mother had never been a part of my life. And for many years that tactic worked. I rarely thought of her. A few months before Barbara found me, however, that pretense started to crumble.

I began having dreams about my mother. In one dream I could see her face clearly, as if she were standing before me. She looked exhausted and upset. Tears streamed from her eyes. Then very distinctly I heard her say my name. I woke up in the middle of the night sweating profusely. Why was I having this dream now? I didn't want to think about her. I thought I had moved past my need to feel like my mother loved me and wanted me.

Later that same week I attended our church, and the pastor spoke on forgiveness. Every time the word forgiveness was mentioned, I felt heavier and heavier. My wife noticed my change in countenance, but she didn't understand it. I couldn't explain it to her. I was consumed with the feeling that I would never be complete until I could let go of the hurt.

But, being prideful, I didn't want to acknowledge that I was still in pain. I didn't want to admit that after 40 years of trying to forget, I still felt unloved and abandoned. I didn't know how to forgive; I didn't feel like my mother deserved to be forgiven. I hated her. I despised the woman who had given birth to me. But as a father, I thought, how could I teach my children about forgiveness — or expect my children to forgive me — when I couldn't let go of my own anger?

The dreams about my mother continued. All of them were slightly different, but in each one she told me she loved me. Sometimes I would dream that we were in a room together, and she would just smile at me. She would wrap her arms around me and hold me like a mother holds her newborn son. I had other dreams where we would be running. I could sense fear, as though we were being chased, and she would grab my hand and tell me that everything would turn out okay. And then I would wake up.

Every time I awoke from such a dream, I would lie in bed and try desperately to hold back the tears. I was 55 years old, and I longed for my mother. I had children of my own, and yet all I wanted was to be the child, to be told that I was loved and wanted.

I knew that something had to be done. My wife prayed with me about my desire to reunite with my mother. The prayers provided me with some peace, but I still felt empty and alone. I wanted to know where my mother was and how my two half-sisters were.

So, with the help of my children, I started looking for them. I searched all over the Internet for Helena, my mother; George, her husband; and my two sisters, Georgia and Barbara. For months we scoured the Internet and came up with no leads, just a string of dead ends. The search was going nowhere, and I was becoming more and more despondent. Finally, I gave up in despair.

A few days later, the pastor of our church challenged us to let go of our friends and family members and let God take over. I knew this was something that had to be done in order for me to find peace. I went home and found a picture of my mother and two sisters. The next Sunday I left the picture on the altar at church, having faith that God would hear my prayers.

And now I was talking to my baby sister. Forty years had passed since I had last spoken with her, and here we were reunited!

"Peter? Are you there?" my sister asked.

"Yes," I cried, "yes, I'm here."

"I can't believe I found you!"

"I've been searching for you and Georgia, too…my kids…my kids were helping me to search for you on the Internet, but we couldn't find you, honey. We just couldn't find you," I tried to explain, crying between words.

"Well, I found you instead."

I noticed the children in the living room, watching me intently as I talked and cried. I could see the tears in all of their eyes. My kids knew what this meant to me. They knew this was exactly what I had been praying for all those months.

Still, my thoughts kept returning to my mother. I knew that Barbara had lived with her. She could tell me where my mother was and maybe even how she felt about me. I wanted to ask, but I was petrified. I was afraid I might hear something I wouldn't be able to handle. Finally, I couldn't hold it in any longer.

"Barbara, um, how's Mama?" I asked quietly.

"Oh, Peter," she sighed. "Mama passed away in March. She kept asking for you. Calling out your name. So when she died, I knew I had to find you."

I listened in silence. My mother, the mother I hated, was dead. And I was broken. Empty. Silent tears streamed down my face.

"I see," I managed to whisper.

"But, Peter, Georgia and I are still alive. And we have children! You have nieces and nephews, Peter."

Yes, I had nieces and nephews. My sisters had nieces and nephews. And this was good news. But my mother was dead. That was all I could think about.

An hour later we ended our conversation, promising to talk the next night. Finding my sisters brought great joy. But the joy was overshadowed by the emptiness I felt knowing that I had missed my mother by less than six months.

I sat at the kitchen table and stared down at my hands. My kids remained quiet in the other room. My wife sat next to me, silent. Finally, I looked up and smiled.

"God answered my prayers tonight. Tonight is a night I will never forget," I told them. They all filed into the kitchen to give me a hug.

But later that night as I lay next to my sleeping wife, all I could do was sob. My mother was gone, and I never had the chance to say goodbye. My mother was gone, and I never had the chance to forgive her. My mother was gone, and I never got to hear her say that she was sorry and that she loved me. I was still just a child wanting his mother's love.

————————————————

"So, Barbara, tell me about Mama," I said to my sister over the phone, months after we first found each other.

I had taken a trip to St. Louis, Missouri, to see her and the rest of my new extended family. Even before the St. Louis trip I met my other sister, Georgia, who lived only six hours from our home in Florida. My family was beautiful. They were thriving, loving individuals with lovely children and grandchildren. My sisters and I had missed out on each other's childhoods, but we were making up for lost time. We talked frequently, and I asked every question that came to mind.

"Well, Mama was beautiful, but you know that," Barbara said.

Yes, I did know, but it had been so long ago. I had a few pictures, but what I really wanted to know was the person behind the picture — who was she?

"What was she like?" I asked.

"She was very funny. She liked to laugh. She loved life. After all, she almost lost it in the concentration camp. She never did get over that."

"The concentration camp?" At first I thought Barbara didn't realize what she had said.

"Yes, a concentration camp."

I distinctly remembered my mother giving me a picture when I lived with her. It was a picture of a man in a Nazi uniform. I had always assumed he was my father. For what other reason would she have given me his picture? She and I had never communicated well, so I couldn't be absolutely certain he was my father. But no other explanation made sense. And if he were my father, then I knew without a doubt that she wouldn't have been arrested and placed in a concentration camp; he would have protected her from that.

"Barbara, it's impossible for Mama to have been in a concentration camp — she was a German."

"Mama talked to us about it sometimes. She was raised Christian, but her mother was actually Jewish. Pete, she didn't lie to us. She was definitely a prisoner in one of the concentration camps," Barbara insisted.

"Which camp then?" I asked, wanting to stump her. She was actually trying to convince me that my mother had been a prisoner in a Nazi death camp — a Jewish prisoner. First of all, I knew she wasn't Jewish; these were just lies to cover up something in her past. Nothing else made sense. Second, if she were in a concentration camp, then how could she have given birth to me? And how could she have survived the camp itself?

"Stutthof Concentration Camp. She told me stories about having to work with her sister there."

"Stutthof? I've never heard of Stutthof. Did you make that up? Where is it located?"

"I don't know. In Germany. I think she said it was in Germany, near Danzig where she lived. All I know is that she was in a concentration camp. Why would she lie to me like that?" my sister asked indignantly.

I was silent for a moment.

"Peter, she had a number on her arm."

As she said that, my mind flashed back to the first time I met my mother. I was 16 years old. She had shown me her arm. I didn't understand then, but now it made my sister's story seem almost believable.

"Barbara, Mama probably made this up, because she was afraid she would be in trouble with the authorities if they found out she was linked to any Nazis," I responded in denial.

"Peter, she told me that you were born in the concentration camp."

The conversation was getting out of hand. There was no way I had been born in a concentration camp. Of course my sister would believe her, but I wasn't going to be so easily duped.

"Barbara, you can believe whatever you want, but this is absolutely the most ridiculous story I've ever heard. I tell you what, if I was born in a concentration camp, then I have a right to know, wouldn't you say?"

"Of course, that's why I told you."

"Good, then I'm going to check up on this story of yours and ask for information from the American Red Cross. We'll see what they find. My guess is they won't find anything," I said.

"Fine. Do what you want. I'm telling you, though, Mama wasn't lying."

We hung up the phone. How in the world could I have been born in a concentration camp? It didn't make any sense. I didn't know much about my mother, but I knew she was no victim. She was the perpetrator. She was the person to blame. My mother was an excuse maker, pure and simple.

She grew up in Germany, fell in love with a Nazi soldier, got pregnant, and then abandoned me. That's what I had told myself all of these years. I held on to that truth. How could all of this have happened while she was a prisoner in a camp? My sisters believed everything my mother told them, but I knew better. I knew not to trust. After all, she was the one who taught me not to trust anyone, especially those closest to you.

I needed to prove to everyone, including myself, that I was right. I needed direct evidence. I found the phone book hidden under a mess of papers on our kitchen counter. The nearest American Red Cross was in Lake City, half an hour from our house. I dialed the number and began the search for my past.

——————————————————

"Mr. Loth, this is Maryann from the American Red Cross," a woman said over the phone. "I have some information for you regarding the request you made."

It had been several months since I first contacted the American Red Cross. I listened with excitement, sure that the information I was about to receive would prove my sisters wrong.

"Mr. Loth, you may want to sit down for this."

There was something about the waver in her voice that concerned me. I grabbed one of our flimsy kitchen chairs and sat down.

"I'm sitting."

"Good. Well, after much searching, we were able to find your mother's records."

There was a slight pause before she continued. "Um, your mother, Helena Loth, was arrested on March 1, 1943, by the Gestapo and placed in Stutthof Concentration Camp."

My throat went dry. I tried hard to swallow, but I ended up coughing instead. I struggled to understand what the woman had just said. This was not what I intended to hear.

"Mr. Loth? Are you all right?" Maryann asked, concerned.

I tried to pull myself together, but the coughing continued. I stood up to get some water, but my legs went out beneath me, causing me to plummet back into the chair.

"Mr. Loth?"

"I'm sorry," I managed to say rather weakly. "I, well, this was not the information I expected. Are you sure you have the right person?"

"I'm afraid so."

"But, my mother wasn't Jewish," I tried to explain, still resisting the full scope of what Barbara had told me.

"Mr. Loth, all we know was that she was arrested." There was another pause before she proceeded. "We also have her prisoner number."

"Her number?" I asked, confused.

"Yes, the number that was tattooed on her arm. Would you like to have it?"

I hesitated. The information about her being a German Jew I could rationalize as some sort of mistake, but having an actual number was a whole different story. While I could hardly believe what I was hearing, I knew I needed to have that number.

"Yes, give it to me."

As she recited my mother's prisoner number, I jotted it down on a napkin at the kitchen table. This couldn't be happening. What this woman was telling me just couldn't be the truth. But if it was, then where did it leave me? Had I been lied to my entire life?

"Mr. Loth, I know you also made a request to look for any information regarding yourself. As of right now, we have been unable to locate any documents relating to you. As I'm sure you are well aware, much has been lost from that time. We will continue to search, however."

I felt somewhat relieved. I didn't need any further information at the moment. I had enough to deal with.

"Do you have any further questions, Mr. Loth?" Maryann asked kindly.

I could think of nothing, my mind a muddled mess.

"No, I don't think so," I replied.

"I'm so sorry, Peter." For the first time, she called me by my first name. I knew she felt sorry for me. I did too.

As I hung up the phone, the enormity of what had just been given to me seemed to smother the life inside of me. The kitchen walls closed in on me as I held the napkin on which I had written my mother's concentration camp number. Looking at the numbers, I tried to imagine them being someone's phone number or social security number. But they weren't, and I knew it. They meant so much more.

And though the information changed much of what I had come to believe about my mother, I still couldn't help but feel that even if she had been in a concentration camp, she never should have abandoned me. She shouldn't have left me an orphan in Poland. I deserved a better life. If nothing else, I deserved to have known the truth. Here I was, 55 years old, and I was just learning that my mother had been arrested and placed in a concentration camp.

As I sat there and did the math, I realized that she was already pregnant with me when she was arrested. Barbara had said I was born in the concentration camp, but I never actually believed it. The reality began to sink in: *I was a Holocaust survivor*. Since Barbara had been right about the concentration camp, then maybe she was right about my mother being Jewish, too. And if my mother was a Jew, then so was I. How many more twists and turns could there be in my life? I felt on edge with the possibility that there was information I still didn't know.

Questions swirled through my mind as I tried to come to grips with all I had learned thus far. There was one question I had asked myself my entire life: who was my father? And now, as I realized that my mother was pregnant with me when she was arrested, I had to ask that question again.

What became of my father? How was it that I never learned his name? How did my parents meet? Were they truly in love with each other? I could only guess. I could only dream up scenarios where my father and mother were lovers, perhaps even engaged to be married, when war broke out and Jews all over Germany and across Europe were being condemned and arrested. I wanted to believe my parents fought hard to stay together. I wanted to know that my father did his best to keep my mother from harm and that despite his efforts the Führer and his army were just stronger.

But why dream up scenarios? What purpose did they serve? They certainly weren't based upon fact. Yet something within me felt compelled to create the stories, to romanticize their relationship. I had to believe in something. If I didn't, I would once again become that little lost orphan boy in Poland.

The reality was that I didn't know truth from fiction. I had been told so many different stories and believed so many of my own made-up stories that I didn't know the difference between the two.

I paced around the kitchen before settling back in the flimsy old chair. As I sat in the deafening silence that reverberated throughout my home, the disjointed pieces of my past began to fall into place in my mind. I started to understand why my childhood had been so confusing, so hurtful. My mind flashed back to Poland as I reflected on the mother who gave me life and how different she was from the mother who saved me from death.

Chapter 1

I grew up in Toruń, Poland, a beautiful town situated near the Wisła (Vees-wa) River. I was only four or five in 1948, but I still vividly remember those early impressions. World War II had just ended, and most of Europe was in shambles. Millions had been murdered during the war — Jews, Poles, Germans, gypsies, and anyone else who seemed to disagree with the Nazi regime.

The Big Three — the United States, Britain, and the Soviet Union — took it upon themselves to change the borders when Germany surrendered and gave up control of Poland. Areas of Germany became Poland, while other sections of Poland became part of the Soviet Union. To bring order to the chaos, elections were held in 1947. However, as so many Eastern European countries experienced at that time, the Communists took complete control through rigged elections. The Polish people were told that the country had been "liberated" by the Soviets, but liberation translated into oppressive Soviet soldiers occupying Polish towns.

I didn't understand all of the politics in 1948, but I could see that the city of Toruń was in complete disarray. Bombed-out buildings dotted the landscape. Crumbling fortress walls surrounded the once beautiful town. Polish currency lost all value, to the point that we used our paper money as toilet paper. There was no electricity, and only one or two stores actually sold food. Periodically, a truck would come by with water, which became our saving grace. Everyone in town would run out to the truck carrying little buckets. We'd fill them to the brim, carrying them carefully back to our homes without spilling. When we were really lucky, we took baths in the public showers, although this treat was reserved for special occasions as it cost money most of us didn't have. Our town certainly wasn't a pretty sight, but I loved it.

I loved it because it was home. And I thought I was rich, because I had a mother who loved me. My matka's name was Julianna Szczepańska (Sh-cha-pine-ska). She was everything to me. Her warm smile could brighten the worst of days.

Already in her mid-forties, Matka was much older than the other mothers of children my age. But no one would know it from the amount of energy she had. She had a way about her that was difficult to ignore. She was of medium height and build, but heads turned when she walked by. Her presence always commanded attention. Perhaps it was her willful spirit that attracted people. But for me, it was the twinkle in her eye when she looked at me that made me feel like the most important person in her life.

Together we lived in a basement in one of the many bombed-out buildings. Our home was unique due to its close proximity to the sewer system. In truth, we lived right next to it. If I looked out our one little window, I could see the sewer. The running water even became a comforting sound as we went to bed each night.

Our home was small and certainly not the coziest place I've ever lived. We had one room, which we divided in half with a blanket. On one side was a little kitchen with a stove; on the other side sat the makeshift bed we shared at night. Even in those tight quarters, though, we were never alone — there were always two or three rats crawling around the floor. Mildew covered the lone window and spread across the wall, feeding off the moisture from the sewer system. Sometimes when I was bored, I would run my fingernails across the green and white growth and try to scratch it off the wall.

The chill stands out most vividly in my memories of our little home. We constantly shivered, trying to wipe away the goose bumps from our legs. The frigid weather made regular bathing impossible, so we sponged ourselves down at night to avoid smelling too strongly the next morning. After our nightly ritual, Matka and I would climb into bed together, snuggling beneath the green army blankets from the Red Cross. When we snuggled up to each other, I was always so much warmer.

While we spent our nights trying to stay warm, we spent many of our days waiting in line for food. One of my earliest memories is standing in line with my matka as we anxiously awaited our daily allotment of food.

Looking back on my living situation now, I can see how dismal it was. At the time it was all I knew. Despite what our home and our lives lacked, I always felt safe. I needed security more than anything, and Matka always tried her best to provide that for me.

— — — — — — — — — — — — — — — — —

"Piotr...Piotr," my matka said, calling me by my Polish name. "Piotr, hurry! We have to get in line before the crowd comes. Put your clothes on, and let's get our wagon together."

I reluctantly left the warmth of our bed. I wanted to wait in the food line with Matka, because it was always so interesting. But I also wanted more sleep.

"Come on, Piotr!" my matka cried.

"I'm coming, I'm coming."

I put on my shirt and some pants and went to find the wagon. The wagon was an important part of our venture for food. We were never certain what might be given to us each day, so the wagon came in handy on those rare days of abundance. I lived for those days. If Matka had the right ingredients, she could make the most delicious soups, filling our little room with mouth-watering smells. Even thinking about it could make my stomach start grumbling.

"Okay, little man, are you set?" Matka asked as she grabbed some blankets off the bed. She walked over to me and smiled. "I don't know what I would do without you. You're my best helper."

I smiled back at her as she wrapped a blanket around me to keep me warm. I knew my matka meant what she said. We were a team, the two of us.

We headed out of the house and met the brisk morning air. It was only 5 o'clock, so the town was still dark. We saw people quietly leaving the warmth of their homes to wait in the food line, and we immediately quickened our pace to avoid being at the end of the line.

We ran down the cobblestone streets of the town, pulling the wagon closely behind us. It bumped up and down on every crack between the stones and rubbed up against my heels. It hurt, but I had no time to pause for pain. Matka and I were on a mission. Sometimes if we arrived too late, there wouldn't be any food left.

Once we arrived just in time to be given the last of the bread and milk. As we walked away, a woman and three of her children came up asking for food. The man handing out food explained that there was none left. She pleaded, but he had nothing to give her.

Matka heard their conversation and turned around. She walked boldly up to the man, looked him straight in the eye, and then handed the woman half of our loaf of bread and all of our milk. The woman graciously thanked her and kissed her hand, but Matka never stopped staring at the man. She didn't say a word, but I could see the man grow uncomfortable. While he may not have had extra food to hand out, we all knew he was given additional rations for his family as pay for handing out the provisions. After a long enough glare, Matka turned around and headed for home with a lighter load.

I hoped today we wouldn't experience a similar encounter. When we finally arrived in the market square, a crowd of people had already gathered. I sighed, happy not to be running anymore, but upset that we hadn't arrived sooner. I pulled the wagon up next to Matka and climbed in, rustling around as I wrapped the blanket fully around me. The morning air was still cool.

As I sat there watching the people standing in line, I tried to guess their names. There was an old man standing in the distance leaning on a cane. He looked like he was one hundred years old. His hands were crippled and worn much like a carpenter Matka knew in town. I guessed his name to be Jozef. In my mind, all carpenters should be named Jozef. Regardless of his name, the man fascinated me. He was so weathered he could barely stand. And beside him was a young girl about my age with golden hair and pretty blue eyes. She held the old man's free hand tightly. I guessed her name was Ańia.

I watched the old man and the little girl for some time before becoming distracted by the woman in front of us. She had a crying baby and was desperately trying to calm him. She kept whispering to him and rocking him back and forth. The rocking motion of the two mesmerized me. The baby, for whatever reason, could not be consoled. Matka smiled at me and stepped toward the woman. She touched the baby's cheek with the backside of her hand and gently whispered something I couldn't hear. The baby purred and was quiet. My matka was always fixing everything.

"Piotr, I remember when you were a baby. You were so beautiful. I knew I would do anything for you."

"Anything?" I asked.

"Of course, anything."

"Then can we have some bacon?" I loved bacon more than anything else — besides candy, of course.

"We'll see," she answered, smiling.

Matka always said, "We'll see." I never got a full answer from her. But she smiled at me and tousled my hair, so I knew if today turned out to be a good food day, I would smell the wonderful aroma of cooking bacon this afternoon.

— — — — — — — — — — — — — —

I must have fallen asleep in the wagon, because by the time it was our turn to receive food it had been several hours. I felt nearly starved. I climbed out of the wagon, which Matka had been tugging along with me in it, and dropped my blanket to the side. I wanted to make sure I was a help to Matka. Plus, I wanted to be close to the food. The man handing out the food sneered at me as I leaned closer to the table to inspect what was being distributed.

"Move back, *Niemiec*," he called to me. "Madam, please tell that child to step out of the way."

"Piotr," she said sternly, causing me to move quickly from my spot. The man seemed to forget my existence as soon as I moved, handing my matka the provisions with a smile.

I knew what *niemiec* meant, because adults in my town often used it when they talked about me. But I couldn't understand why they called me a "German." After all, I lived in Poland like the rest of them. The sneer that accompanied the word confused me even more. I once asked Matka about it, but she told me not to worry and sent me out to play. I forgot about it for the time being, but the ugly word always seemed to resurface.

At home, I helped Matka unload the wagon. Then I climbed back into bed as she began cooking. I liked to lie there and watch her use what little we were given to make a feast.

My matka had a systematic way of cooking. First she chopped down the bacon into tiny pieces. Then she fried it up in a frying pan until it became very crispy. She always gave me a few little pieces as a treat. Then she chopped some onion and fried that with the bacon pieces. When she set the mixture out on the window sill, it turned into pure white grease that we spread on our bread like butter. I never had anything so delicious. Even today my mouth waters for the taste of that spread.

After frying up the bacon, Matka would take the milk and boil it. She separated the cream on top from the milky water found beneath it. She placed the milky water on the window sill until it soured and then poured sugar over it. Later, she would give it to me as dessert.

Matka always kept a few of the bones she was given to put in our soup, but she took the rest and traded them for vegetables like potatoes and beets. These she cut up and put in the soup she always had stewing on the stove. We were never without soup. Soup was our saving grace, because it was the one food we could always keep going. Our stove was always on, and it always had a pot of soup over it. That stove was wonderful because it served two purposes: keeping us fed and keeping us warm.

As I lay there in bed watching my matka, I felt warm and cozy. I could have stayed there all day long. She was so intent on her cooking that she barely paid any attention to me — at least for a few minutes.

"Piotr, get up. Don't be lazy. It will be a few hours before our dinner. Go outside and play," she said as she set the milk on the window sill to sour.

Though I would have been perfectly content to stay in bed and watch Matka, I obeyed her with little hesitation. Besides, I loved playing outside, even if it was a little chilly. Sometimes other kids would join me, but I didn't need other kids to have fun. My home was a playground.

The city of Toruń was founded by the Teutonic Knights in 1233 and soon became a major port of trade due to its prime location on the Wisła River. In order to protect the town from menacing intruders, the knights built a fortress around the town limits. There were several gates and entryways, and near the main gate stood a tall tower. Within the fortress, they built a castle as a dwelling for the nobles, but in 1454 the town's citizens rebelled against the knights' rule and destroyed the castle. The only part of the castle still standing was a latrine tower, which was built over a stream — the same stream that served as the sewer next to our home. Our home was located right between what was left of the castle and the remaining fortress walls that surrounded our city.

Unfortunately, the fortress walls did little to keep out the Soviets who now occupied our town. I put them to my own uses, however. One of my favorite things to do when not watching Matka cook was to try to climb up a portion of the fortress walls. I spent hours strategizing a way to successfully climb it, but I had yet to succeed. I desperately wanted to make it to the top, but it was a big ambition for a five year old.

First, I had to come up with a different strategy. How was I going to get up the entire wall without falling like I normally did? The problem was that the wall didn't have as many stepping stones as I needed. The easiest path seemed to be a rare type of ladder made of stones, which led to a flat board that served as a covering of some sort. Once on top of the board, I would have to figure out a way to climb up the rest of the wall, which consisted of flat brick all the way to the top. I had tried this tactic before and only managed to fall back onto the board, but this time I felt more determined. I would make it up the wall if I died trying.

I ran toward the 12-foot wall and jumped up onto the first step. By the third stone step, I slipped and ended up back on the ground. Whoever made the steps obviously didn't intend on someone like me climbing the wall, but I was stubborn and intent on making it to the top.

I started again, this time holding on to the step above me for support. As I placed each foot on a new stone, I also grabbed a higher step for support. If my matka saw me she would have called me a *maupa* — a monkey — and rung my neck. But she wasn't there, so I wasn't worried.

I managed to reach the board and pull myself up onto it. That was the hard part. I was certainly light enough, but I wasn't the strongest child ever to climb up the fortress wall. I sat on the board for a moment and caught my breath. Climbing was fun, but tiring.

A little bird landed near my feet and stood there cocking its head a little to the right in order to keep its eye on me. I watched it closely. I envied the little creature. It would never be able to climb up the wall, but its wings enabled it to glide ever so gently and land on the very board that had taken me so long to reach. I moved my feet, and the bird flew up and over the fortress wall. I wished I could just as easily fly to the top, but I knew that eventually I'd make it. Once I did, I'd literally be on top of the world.

I pulled myself upright, standing confidently on the board. I was over halfway up the structure. If only I could find some grooves for my hands and feet, but I didn't see any as I looked up the wall. Undaunted, I placed myself flat against the wall and jumped up to a spot where a brick was jutting out. I grabbed the edge of it with my right hand and slid my feet along the wall, hoping to catch some unseen groove to boost myself higher. There was nothing.

Instead, my hand slipped, and I went tumbling back down onto the board. I tried to catch myself from following the downward angle of the board, but I had fallen so hard that the weight of my body pulled me toward the ground. As I went over the side of the board, I instinctively reached for the stepping stones. I was able to grab one, and I dangled there for a moment before I found my footing on a stepping stone beneath me. My heart was beating so fast, I could hardly breathe.

Slowly I made my way down to the ground and looked at my hands. My palms were bruised, and blood trickled from a couple of my fingertips where I had tried to grab the bricks. My stomach bore all kinds of scratches, too. It was time to go home. Besides, dinner was almost ready. I knew that tomorrow would be a new day for climbing.

————————————————

That night I went to bed with a full stomach. My arms ached from my afternoon climb, but the scratches didn't bother me. I was snuggled up in bed with my matka, and I was tired. In no time, I was fast asleep.

Bang! Bang! Bang!

Matka jumped out of bed, scaring me half to death.

"Mamusiu, what is it?" I cried.

She looked frightened. This was not the matka who was normally in control.

"Shhhhh, Piotr. It's okay," she said as she lit a candle and walked over to the door.

Bang! Bang!

The noise was even louder as Matka took her time answering the door. I quickly crawled beneath the covers. My body began to shake as I watched her through a hole in the blanket. I tried to calm myself, but between the fear and the cold wind that swirled in our house as Matka opened the door, there was nothing I could do. Standing in the entryway were two Soviet soldiers armed with guns.

I was used to seeing Soviet soldiers around town. Most of them seemed to despise being stationed in Poland. It was especially apparent that the Soviet soldiers and the Polish police disliked one another. The Polish police were given the most menial of jobs as a way to taunt them and put them in their "proper" place as lower-class citizens. And because the Soviets were in power, the Polish officers were required to follow their orders or else face severe repercussions.

But the distaste toward Polish people didn't stop with the Polish police; the Soviet soldiers hated all Poles, believing we were all beneath them in social status. On several occasions I had witnessed the way they taunted and criticized individuals for no apparent reason. And I had heard stories of the Soviets going to homes in the

31

middle of the night to terrorize people, but I never expected them at my doorway.

"Julianna Szczepańska?" one of them asked in a stern voice.

"Yes," Matka responded.

"These papers here show us that you have a German child in your possession." The taller man thrust the papers at Matka. The other soldier pushed past her and entered our room. He walked swiftly to the bed where I hid shivering.

"You know this child doesn't belong here with you. Why do you have him when he clearly belongs with the other children like him? We're taking him with us," said the approaching soldier as he threw the covers off the bed.

"Get up, child!" he yelled to me in Polish so that I could understand. I started crying. I didn't want to get up. I wanted to sleep. I wanted to remain in the warmth of my bed with Matka.

"Quit crying and get up!" he screamed as he towered over me.

My matka ran over to the man and clutched his arm, crying. "Please, please, don't take him. He is my child. He is my son."

"Madam, please, don't make this any more difficult," the taller soldier said from the doorway.

I didn't respond to the men. I just lay there crying, hoping they would go away. The soldier at the bed grabbed me by the arm and yanked me up. I screamed louder but that didn't deter him.

My matka ran over and held on to me as the man tried to lift me up.

"No, please don't take him away. Please!" she cried as he lifted me up and away from her.

The men ignored her cries and walked toward the door. The one carrying me told me to shut up, but I continued to scream, kick, and cry. I didn't want to leave my matka. I didn't want to go with these men. Why were they taking me away? I didn't understand.

"Mamusiu!" I screamed.

"Please! Let me go with him. I can go with him," she pleaded with the men.

The soldier put me down and consulted the taller soldier in Russian. I quickly ran over to Matka. I tried to ask her what was happening, but I could barely speak I was sobbing so hard.

"Shhhh, Piotr. Mamusia is here. I will take care of you," she calmed me through her own tears.

My nose was all runny, and I struggled to see through my tears. I buried my head into Matka's robe. She gently stroked my head as she whispered a prayer in my ear. I didn't know this God to whom she was speaking, but I desperately hoped He would answer my matka's fervent prayers.

The soldiers kept glancing over at us as they talked. They made me nervous, so I held on to Matka even tighter. She clutched me back. After some time, the soldiers approached us.

"Madam, you will go with us. Take the boy, and walk ahead of us. And please, madam, don't do anything stupid."

My matka cried a sigh of relief.

"Oh, thank you. Thank you. I will go with him." She turned to me and held my face in her hands. "Come, Piotr. We must be brave and go on an adventure. Would you like to go on an adventure?"

To please her, I nodded yes. Deep down inside, I was petrified. If this was an adventure, I didn't want any part of it.

"Come, we must go," barked the taller soldier.

Matka grasped my hand tightly and began to hum a tune as we walked. At first I was scared the officers would yell at her, but they didn't seem to mind her soft voice. She had a beautiful voice, even though she was only humming. My whole body relaxed. Suddenly this adventure didn't seem as scary as I had first imagined. Yes, there were Soviet soldiers with guns behind me. But in the end, I had my matka. My matka was with me, and everything would be fine.

Even with that confidence, I felt compelled to turn around and take quick surveys of the Soviet soldiers. They were powerful looking men with stern faces. Even their dark green uniforms and matching green hats seemed stern. Every time I stole a glance at them, shivers shot up my spine. Who were these men, and what did they want with us?

"Mamusiu, where are we going?" I finally asked her. Most of my tears had dried, and I felt much calmer. She stopped humming and faintly smiled at me.

"Don't worry so much, Piotr. We're going on an adventure."

As she was talking to me, the Soviet soldiers drew closer and ordered us to go straight ahead to the train station. I hadn't noticed that we had walked so far. The train station stood at the outskirts of town, and we were only a short distance from the tracks.

The train station was completely deserted. I watched as the taller of the two Soviet soldiers conversed with the man in the ticket booth. The elderly gentleman appeared flustered as he hurriedly wrote out a ticket and provided the soldier with change. The Soviet soldier looked bored.

"Come, let's proceed to the platform," the soldier standing near me said as he motioned us toward the stairs.

The short staircase went up through a dark passageway. As we reached the top of the stairs, the Soviet soldier lightly pushed aside a set of double doors. We were back outside in the brisk night air, waiting on a platform for a train to take us to some unknown destination. Wherever it was going, I knew I didn't want to be on that train.

"Sit here, child," the soldier commanded as he pointed to a wooden bench on the platform. He stood next to me, staring ahead.

The taller soldier emerged from the station booth and motioned for my matka to come before him. I watched as they talked in the distance.

"Why am I here?" I cried to the soldier standing near me, hoping he would answer. He didn't.

I turned back toward where my matka was standing. I could see that she was upset by the way she stood. A new worry stirred within me. I slid my hands in between the wooden slats on the bench and clenched them tightly.

It was the middle of the night. No one was around but the four of us. What was going on? And why did they say I was a German child?

Unable to answer the questions, I looked up into the sky. Right above us the moon was shining brightly. I had never seen a moon so round and full. The night was completely still, and there wasn't a cloud in the sky.

Matka finally walked over and sat beside me. She held me tightly and kept rocking me back and forth. I slowly let go of my grip on the slats and wrapped my arms around her. We sat together in silence, finding comfort in the light of the moon.

A few moments later, I heard a train in the distance. My eyes left the night sky as I watched the bright lights of the train cross over the Wisła River toward our station. Matka grasped me tighter as it approached. The noise of the screeching wheels grew louder until the train finally halted in front of us. Several passengers ambled off the train, their eyes heavy with recent sleep. They hardly noticed us as they made their way to the double doors. I wished I were one of them, going home to my own bed.

The two Soviet soldiers approached us from where they were standing a short distance away, talking. The taller one gave my matka a look. She turned toward me, taking my hand and clasping it to her chest.

"Piotr, you are going on this train without me. I can't go with you, because this is your very own adventure. I know right now you are feeling frightened, but you must be brave for me. I promise I will come and get you." She held me tightly and kissed me, crying softly. "I will find you, and I will bring you back home safe and sound."

"No, Mamusiu, I don't want to go," I cried as the shorter soldier grabbed my arm and guided me toward the train.

My feet felt heavy as we made our way to the edge of the platform. I wanted them to become like heavy weights, so the Soviet soldier wouldn't be able to move me. But he was too strong. He picked me up, and I hung limply at his side. Only when he got to the side of the train did he put me down so that I could walk for myself.

I looked behind me as I sadly ascended the steps up into the train, but the soldier pushed me ahead so that I could catch only a glimpse of Matka. The soldier gave my ticket to the train conductor and led me down the narrow aisle to our seats. He allowed me to sit by the window, and I peered out onto the platform where my matka stood.

"Mamusiu!" I yelled, waving my hands back and forth to get her attention. She waved back at me and stepped closer to the train.

I heard the rumble of the engine as it started. The train's wheels churned. I continued waving and crying, watching my matka the entire time. I could see her mouth moving, trying to tell me something, but the noises of the train drowned out her voice.

"Mamusiu, I love you!" I screamed with all my might.

But the train had started moving by then, and she couldn't hear me. I made sure to keep my eyes on her as we pulled away from the station. From the light of the big moon I could see the tears streaming down her face.

My matka loved me. She didn't want me to go either. I sobbed quietly to myself before falling fast asleep.

Chapter 2

"Wake up, child," a rough voice said, invading my dreams. I didn't like the sound of the voice at all. I wanted this dream to end. Or maybe, I thought to myself, I should wake up and know that I am safe in Matka's bed. I slowly opened my eyes.

"Get up!" barked the voice again, this time accompanied by hands pulling me out of my seat.

Before me stood a different soldier than the one I had fallen asleep next to a few hours earlier. For a moment I longed for the other soldier, for a somewhat familiar face. But from where I sat, I saw no sign of him. The new soldier glared at me and cursed under his breath. My heart pounded in my chest. I wasn't at home. I wasn't safe with Matka. I could feel the tears well up in my eyes.

"Stand up, boy! We're getting off this train." The soldier grabbed my arm and thrust me into the middle of the aisle. Ahead I could see other children being ordered off the train as well.

Even though I had just woken up, I was alert and willing to obey out of pure fear. As we stepped onto the platform of the Grudziądz (Grew-jones) train station, we were immediately directed toward a horse and wagon. I joined a line of children waiting for their turn to get into one of the two wagons sitting outside the station.

"Listen," hollered a man driving one wagon, "we are taking you to the orphanage. You are unwanted children. Your parents are dead or don't want you anymore. Since you've got no other place to go, we're going to help you out. So ride quietly like good children, and there won't be any trouble."

The man's words paralyzed me with fear. I had never heard of an orphanage. And from the sound of it, I didn't belong with this group of kids. After all, he said they were unwanted. I knew for a fact that I was wanted. My matka loved me. She didn't want me to go. Why would they take me away from her?

The first wagon was full of children by the time I arrived, so I headed toward the second one. There were already several children waiting quietly on the floorboards. They stared in silence as I found a seat between two boys. I didn't want to look at any of them. These were unwanted children, and I was in the wrong place.

"Get situated, because we aren't stopping for anything," the wagon driver informed us as he got up into his seat.

I sat in silence as we slowly made our way up a long dirt road into a small town called Białochowo (Bee-ya-wa-hovo). We bumped along, knocking knees and heads as we rode. On either side of us were trees that seemed to go on forever. Above us were a million stars. The road was dark from the shadows of the trees, so the stars illuminated the way for us. I stared up at them, wondering what Matka was doing. Was she sleeping now? Was she missing me?

On either side of me sat two older boys. Their bodies warmed me as we traveled down the desolate road. Neither one said a word to me, even though I couldn't keep the tears from falling from my eyes.

After some time we pulled off the main road and headed down a dirt path with fruit trees on either side of it. They were beautiful apple and cherry trees. My mouth watered as I thought of the delicious fruit dangling just meters from where we drove. If only I could reach out and grab one as we drove past. Before I could even stand up and try, however, we pulled up in front of a white villa. It was a large, beautiful home with whitewashed walls and huge windows looking out over the driveway.

As we pulled up closer to the house, some of the children came alive with bursts of energy. Several of them started talking excitedly and others began to hum or sing, but I stayed put. I refused to be pleased to be there just because the building was pretty. After a few moments, the wagon drivers ordered several of the children to start filing out of the wagon. The two boys next to me began to climb out of our wagon, so I followed them. Though no words had been spoken between us during the whole drive, I felt safe with them.

"You!" a Soviet soldier pointed at me as I began to descend from the wagon. "Get back in the wagon. We're taking you down the road."

Frightened by the soldier's tone of voice, I made my way back to my spot, though I desperately wanted to be near those boys. Even though there were other children in the wagon with me, I felt unsettled by the separation.

Those of us who did remain were silent. There was no excited laughter or talking. There was no humming or singing. Fear gripped me as I sat there. I wanted to be with those other children who were now running around in the yard. There was something calming about their noisy chatter, something we lacked in the silence of our wagon.

After more than half of the children had unloaded from the wagons, the remaining children were ushered into my wagon to be hauled off to a smaller building down the road. The second building was white like the villa we had just left, but it looked like the paint had been peeling for years. Its one redeeming quality was that it sat peacefully on a nicely sized lake.

"Okay, now it's your turn to get out. Get in an orderly line, please," said the driver.

We each got down from the wagon and headed toward the house. We filed into the small building one by one. A woman led us to a room upstairs where there were already boys and girls sleeping on the floor.

"This is where you will be sleeping. You might as well get comfortable now. There's an hour left before chores start in the morning," the woman explained.

She handed us uniforms to change into and told us to go to sleep quickly. I looked around at the children in the room. Between the new arrivals and those already sleeping, there were about twenty of us. We each hesitantly put on the gray uniforms and tried to find a place to sleep. The floor was covered with children. I found a spot near a wall and curled up tight. The floor was hard and cold, so I huddled closer to the girl beside me. As I tried to fall asleep, all I could think of was my matka and our warm bed in Toruń.

I awoke to the smell of urine. One of the latrine buckets in the middle of the room had toppled over during the night, and the stench stung my nostrils. I pulled myself up and saw a little girl sitting beside me. She smiled shyly at me. She wore a plain gray uniform like me, but being a girl she wore a skirt instead of pants. A faded yellow star was stitched to her shirt. Some of the stitches were coming out, so the star hung limply off her chest. For some reason, all I could focus on was that star.

"Children! Come, we will eat some breakfast, and then we will go work in the fields," commanded the stern woman who met us when we first arrived. We stretched and followed the woman down the stairs to a room that smelled of warm bread.

"Grab a slice and move on so others can have a chance to eat!" she yelled above the chatter of the other children. I felt too shy to participate in the conversation. I was more interested in the food being offered. My stomach grumbled in anticipation.

The bread was warm and tasty. I hadn't eaten in many hours, and it felt good to satisfy my hunger pains. The little brown-haired girl with the star sat beside me on the floor.

"My name is Piotr," I told her.

"Hi, Piotr," she answered shyly.

She may have told me her name, but over the years I have forgotten it. I will never forget the nickname I had for her, however. I asked her once if I could call her *Gwiazda*, the Polish word for star. She smiled and said that was a very pretty name. From then on, Star went wherever I went. We were inseparable. She was my very first friend.

For months Star and I worked together doing various chores. Sometimes the people running the orphanage, our wardens, sent us out into the field to pick sugar beets, and we would throw them onto wagons to be taken into town and be sold. Other times we were told to clean the floors of the orphanage or wash the dirty clothes that had accumulated over several weeks. We washed the clothes by hand, raking them across the washing board. We did our best to scrub them down with soapy water, but the soap wasn't strong enough to eliminate all of the stains and smells.

Star and I completed our chores by making up little songs and games. She would teach me songs she had learned at other orphanages, and then we would make up our own songs to sing. We had the most fun together at the end of the day when all of our chores were complete. We would run by the lake and try to catch the little fish. I was better at catching them than she was, so she would cup her hands and hold the ones I caught. She always laughed and laughed when the little fish wiggled. She said it tickled her hands.

We also ran around the lake and out into the fields where the big barns were that held farming tools and some of the sugar beets we had picked. I would hide between bales of crops, and Star would come find me. Sometimes it took her too long, so I would jump out and scare her when she passed my hiding spot. Other children joined us, but Star was my best friend. She made me laugh, and she comforted me when I was scared and missed my matka.

One day after several months at the orphanage, our wardens allowed us to visit the other orphanage down the road to watch a film. The twenty of us grimy children trudged down the little dirt road, humming the songs we had made up in the fields. As we turned the corner and entered the gates of the other orphanage, I was struck by its immense size. I had forgotten how much larger and more beautiful the villa was in comparison to the little house where we stayed.

Our wardens led us into the building, where we were met by the very same children who had taken the wagon ride with us months earlier. Now there was a distinct difference between us. Their clothes were bright and clean; ours were dirty and gray. They also seemed better fed, even a little plump. We, on the other hand, looked like we were wasting away. As I observed these differences, I noticed out of the corner of my eye the two boys whom I had sat beside on our long journey to this place. I smiled at them, but they didn't seem to remember me.

As the adults steered us down the corridor toward the stairs, I found that the inside of the orphanage was just as beautiful as the outside. Most of the children trotted up the stairs to the room where they were going to show the film, but I ventured off alone when no one was looking. Curious about what the rest of the house looked like, I entered a room to the left of the stairs. The room was long, with a huge dining table and many chairs situated around it. Behind the table were large glass windows. I looked out onto the little winding road on which we had traveled when we first arrived in the wagons. As I stood near the window, all I could think of was escaping. If I were to run down that road, would I be able to run all the way to Matka?

"Child! What are you doing? Come watch the film with the others," a woman with a kind voice said, awakening me from my daydream. I followed her up the stairs and into the room where all the wide-eyed children watched the film. Star was sitting in the back corner, so I made my way to the back and sat beside her on the floor to watch the film.

For the first time in my life, I was able to enter a world wholly different than my own. I wanted to jump inside the film and live with the cowboys and Indians. Forget living in Poland at an orphanage — I wanted to live in America.

When the movie finished, those of us who lived at the smaller orphanage were told to wash the floors, while the rest of the children went outside to play. So, twenty little gray soldiers scrubbed the floors of the entire building, upstairs and down.

———————————————

The chores, though tedious and tiring, weren't horrible. At least, they weren't as horrible as the nights. After we had finished our chores and eaten our dinners, we were sent upstairs for bed, which should have been a peaceful time of rest. About once a week, however, some of the wardens would come in the middle of the night and select two boys and two girls to take with them upstairs. At first those of us who weren't chosen had no idea where the children were being taken, but when they came back we didn't want to know. The selected children always came back crying and bleeding. Some bled so badly they could hardly walk. Others sobbed so loudly that I couldn't fall back asleep.

Every night at that orphanage I lay awake, frightened. All I wanted was my matka. I cried along with those children. I cried and cried, "Matka! Come and get me, please! Matka!" Eventually I would fall asleep in the arms of Star, who comforted me.

One night Star and I lay snuggled up together, sleeping after a particularly hard day out in the fields picking sugar beets. Right as we drifted off to sleep, two women came in and woke us up.

"Come on, wake up," the taller woman said to me as she picked me up by the arm. I could smell the nasty aroma of alcohol on her breath. She moved toward another little girl and boy lying near us and woke them as well.

Frightened, the four of us followed the women upstairs and down the hall to the far end of the building. I had never been on that side of the building, so I was curious. The women were laughing softly to one another as they walked ahead of us. The taller one would look behind her from time to time to see that we were still with them.

As we reached the end of the hall, a fear I had never experienced before welled up inside of my chest. I could barely breathe. I looked over at Star, who was holding my hand. She was scared as well, but she smiled at me and squeezed my hand in assurance.

"C'mon! Come into the room. Don't just stand there!" the shorter woman snapped at us as she entered the room at the end of the hall.

Timidly, we walked in and saw three men drinking wine and laughing loudly. They looked us up and down, commenting on how small we were.

"Absolutely darling, aren't they?" the taller woman asked as she laughed and grabbed a glass of wine.

We sat watching the adults drink bottle after bottle of wine. Soon they grew bored with their alcohol and turned to us. The man sitting farthest from us ordered us to take off our clothes. Frightened and embarrassed, none of us moved.

"Make them take off their clothes!" he ordered the man closest to us.

43

We sat there as one by one they stripped us of our clothing. As the women sat back and watched in their drunken stupor, the men began to rape us. And beat us. And then they raped us again. Pain seared my insides. The first man who approached me threw me aside when he was done with me. I could feel the blood trickling from my backside, but I didn't dare move.

As I lay there shaking, I looked over to Star and saw the other two men raping her at the same time. She was screaming and crying for them to stop, but they ignored her pleas. I wanted to help her, but there was nothing I could do. When they were done with her, they turned and raped me, too. I wept and screamed. The pain was unbearable. I kept my eyes on Star the entire time. She huddled in the corner, sobbing uncontrollably. When they were finished with me, I hurried over to the corner where Star sat.

As I shook with pain and fear, I heard the screaming of the other children who had been brought up with us. I couldn't bear to hear the screams, knowing the intense pain they were enduring. I remembered that the other boy was much smaller than me. As my eyes found him in the room, I watched as he cried and screamed with such pain that he eventually passed out.

That didn't stop them from finishing what they had started. They took a break to drink some more before approaching us again. The taller man grabbed me by the arm, ripping me away from my hold on Star. I screamed, but it only made the man angry.

"Quit crying, you little baby!" he yelled, punching me in the stomach and tossing me back to the floor.

They continued to beat us until we bled inside and out. Afterwards one of the women took me aside and made me do things I didn't want to do. She slapped me across the face and called me a baby, because I cried. I couldn't understand the pain. Where was my matka? Why wasn't she there to help me? Did she really love me? Because if she did, why would she let me be taken away to be tortured?

After they finished using us, they returned to their drinking and smoking. The four of us huddled together, quietly crying, as the adults hurled insults at us. Finally, after what seemed like hours, they walked us back to our room.

As I lay beside Star we held each other and cried. I wanted my matka so badly. But Star, who was bleeding in front and back, kept saying, "It will be okay, Piotrusiu. It will be okay." Oh, how I loved her.

The following week my matka came to rescue me. She came in holding papers and demanded that the wardens hand me over to her. They looked over the papers and allowed me to leave. I'm still not sure why, but they also allowed Star to come with us. And so we made our way back to our home in Toruń, where it was safe.

Chapter 3

When we reached my beautiful home of Toruń, I felt completely relieved. I was home with my matka. As we got off the train and crossed the platform where Matka and I had sat together on that night months earlier, I shuddered to think what had occurred in the meantime.

Matka held me by the hand, and I reached out for Star who was behind me. We silently walked out of the station and headed toward our home. On our way there, we stopped at a small apartment on the corner. Matka rang the buzzer, and a woman opened the door. Star and I were quickly ushered inside. We didn't care where we were so long as it wasn't the orphanage.

Star and I sat on the floor and snuggled up to one another as Matka explained to the woman all she had done to get me back. She had resorted to calling up her brother, Franek, an officer in the Polish army. Together, she and Franek obtained the necessary paperwork to get me out of the orphanage. When the women began discussing logistics that I couldn't follow, I dozed off.

After a few hours, Matka woke me up and told me we were going home.

"Piotr, Star will stay here. Let's go home."

I nodded in understanding. I reached over to Star, who was sleeping soundly, and hugged her tightly. She barely even moved. I whispered in her ear, "Goodbye, Star."

Once home, Matka took me into her arms and cried. Tears flowed down her cheeks and trickled onto my face, which was pressed against hers. Her tears made me cry, too. She held me tightly to her chest as we sat together in her rocking chair. She rocked me and cried softly, nuzzling the back of my head.

"Oh, Piotrusiu, I love you. I love you so much. I won't let them take you away. You are my son, no matter what anyone tells you. I love you, I love you, I love you," she whispered gently.

I held her tightly and cried. All the pain I had gone through had been horrible, but I felt safe because my matka loved me. She loved me more than anyone else, and I knew it.

Months passed, and my wounds finally healed. I was able to walk straight again, so I joined the children in playing outside. But my favorite times were when Matka would rock me in her rocking chair. I lived for those times.

———————————————

After three months, there came another knock on the door. Again soldiers ordered us to go with them. They put large boots on my feet and gave me pants and a jacket to wear. Matka was also told to get dressed in nice clothes. Then they walked us to the middle of town where a funeral was taking place. The air was brisk and cold, and I shuddered despite the large jacket draped across my small shoulders. In the crowd I saw Star. We waved to one another from a distance, but there were too many people in the way to approach each other.

"Today is a sad day," a large Polish soldier boomed, his voice echoing across the hushed crowd that had gathered. "One of our men has died from injuries he sustained in the war. So today we will all be partakers in his funeral, which might never have had to take place had it not been for the Jews and the Germans."

I asked Matka who the dead man was. Did we know him? Matka shook her head no. Yet we were being forced to walk across town to the cemetery for his burial.

Since my boots were too big, blisters began to form on the backs of my heels as we walked. We walked for what seemed like miles, and I could think only about the pain in my feet. With every step I took, the backs of the boots rubbed against my already raw skin. I tried not to cry, but my feet were throbbing. Then I saw Star just ahead of us. Temporarily forgetting the soreness in my feet, I prodded Matka to walk faster. Finally, we reached Star, and the two of us embraced. Before I knew it, we were around the corner from the cemetery, and I hadn't thought about my feet since reuniting with Star.

Once inside the cemetery, it became clear why we were a part of this Polish soldier's funeral procession. The Polish soldiers were blaming us for his death. They pointed their fingers at me and Star, as well as some other orphans among the group, and told us we were the cause of this righteous man's death. I couldn't understand their reasoning, but then again, I didn't ever understand adults. They were angry people, and when they set their mind on something, we children had no choice but to obey.

Being so close to death scared me, so I huddled closer to Matka. As I did, a soldier spotted me and grabbed me by the back of my neck.

"Are you scared? Are you frightened by what your father did to our soldiers? You *Niemiec* scoundrel! Kiss the soldier! Kiss him!" he yelled as he pushed me closer to the face of the dead man, whose cold body lay in a sinister-looking black casket.

I screamed as loudly as I could, frightened by the expression on the dead man's face. His eyes were partly open, and his face was ashen white. The soldier, out of disgust, threw me into the casket and shut it, locking it from the outside. I screamed and screamed, petrified of the dead man I was now lying over. I felt like he was looking right at me through his half-open eyes. I could hear Matka yelling at the soldiers, but no one came to my rescue. My voice eventually gave out, but my tears continued to splash onto the face of the dead man beneath me. Every part of my body shook uncontrollably. Finally my bodily functions released, and I passed out.

I don't remember much after that. All I know is that I woke with a start after a soldier poured water on me. Another soldier pulled me out of the casket and handed me a bouquet of flowers, telling me that I could walk out in front of the funeral procession back into town. I think this gesture was meant to appease me for the torture I had just endured. However, being separated from my matka was not what I wanted at that moment. I looked behind me, still shaking from the cold air that penetrated my wet clothes, and saw that Matka and Star weren't too far behind. I whimpered and tried to forget about the dead man I had nearly kissed.

A few weeks after the funeral, I found myself back at the Białochowo orphanage. I could never understand why the soldiers kept coming to our house and ordering me to the train station. "My matka loves me!" I would scream. But they didn't care about a little 6-year-old "orphan" boy. They just followed orders, rounding up all the orphan children, including Star. So we were back at the Białochowo orphanage — picking sugar beets, scrubbing floors, washing dirty laundry, and being abused.

The days were always hot then, and when we worked in the sugar beet fields, I longed to sit in the shade or jump into the little lake by our orphanage. One day as I picked, I stared out beyond the field of sugar beets into an adjoining field of poppies. I looked around and saw that everyone was busy picking within his or her designated row. In the distance I saw the adults huddled together over the water bucket. They were discussing something, which meant no one was watching me. I crouched down low and made my way toward the poppies, slowly moving the stalks this way and that as I crossed the field. I peeked my head just above the stalks to survey the scene. The adults were still off in the distance, so I knew I was safe.

When I reached the field of beautiful red poppies, I knelt down and felt the cool dirt in the shade of the beautiful flowers. I sat for a moment before lying down flat on my back. I gazed up into the sky. It was clear except for a few puffy white clouds off to the right. As I lay there, I began to wonder what Matka was doing at that very moment. For the time being I was at peace, alone in my own world of red poppies, and it felt good.

After my initial escape from my chores, I managed to slip away on several more occasions. The adults never noticed I was missing, but sometimes Star would find me in my field of poppies. We would lie there next to each other, holding hands without saying anything. Nothing needed to be said. She knew I was thinking of Matka. And as we gazed into the sky together, we would just cry. We cried for Matka, we cried from the pain, we cried for each other, and often we just cried to cry. It felt good to let it all out through our tears.

The nights were always the same, however. I would sleep huddled on the floor, hoping with all that was in me that I wouldn't be the one selected that particular evening. When I was overlooked, I sighed in relief — and then felt immense sorrow and guilt for the boys and girls who were selected instead. And when they came back to the room crying and bleeding, I knew that my turn would be coming soon.

One couldn't avoid being selected for long, so I again found myself being led down that same hall to the same room of vile adults. I lost track of how many times I was taken to that hateful room, but each time was like the first. During those horrible moments, I would close my eyes and try to think of Matka. I would try to envision myself in Toruń, climbing our fortress wall or eating Matka's delicious soup. Those little visions never lasted long, though. The pain was just too much.

One night, Star wasn't chosen with me. I was completely alone. Though I was happy she was safe, the loneliness magnified my pain. I could feel the blood trickle down my thighs. And my stomach burned from each thrust against the hard floor. When they were done with us, they ordered me to stand, but that simple task was impossible for me. As much abuse as I had endured, I had never suffered the kind of agony I felt that night. My body was limp from the pain, so one of the men reluctantly picked me up and carried me back to our room.

The next morning one of the women from the night before came in to check on me. I hadn't slept all night. The pain was too severe. I was still bleeding from my backside, and every time I tried to move it felt like something was tearing inside of me. The woman quickly ordered that I be taken to the doctor. Several of the men who worked in the fields came up the stairs to carry me out to the wagon. I couldn't sit, so I had to lie on my stomach as we made our way to the doctor.

On the drive into town I could feel every bump in the dirt road, which sent me reeling in agony. Occasionally the man driving the wagon asked if I was all right, but I never answered him. After a few attempts he gave up asking me. I think he knew it was severe.

Slowly we made our way through one village and into another. The little homes along the side of the road looked so inviting. Outside of one I saw a mother bent low near a child, wiping the dirt off his face with a rag. She kissed him lightly on the nose and resumed hanging her laundry on the clothesline that ran between two trees near her small shack. All the physical pain in the world wouldn't have been as painful as that sight of a loving mother and her son. I cried not because of the physical pain anymore, but because I needed my mother.

We drove into the center of a town and stopped in front of a row of buildings with pretty flowers hanging from the balconies. The wagon driver lifted me from my seat. We entered the first building and were immediately greeted by a friendly, plump woman.

"Good morning! Ooooh, what's wrong with your child?" she purred.

"He's not mine. I just drove him out here from the orphanage. He's in a lot of pain. Can he see the doctor?" the wagon driver responded quickly.

The nurse called for the doctor at once. A tall man approached swiftly, motioning for the wagon driver to follow him into his examining room.

"Do you know what happened to this child?" asked the doctor sternly after examining me.

"No, sir. I was just told to drive him to the doctor. Is it bad?" he asked with concern.

"Well, yes. His rectum is torn and needs to be sewn back together. I'll need your help, as well yours, Basia," he said as he looked at the nurse.

Neither the wagon driver nor the nurse asked how my rectum had been torn. Maybe they knew but didn't want the truth to be confirmed. Or maybe the swift way in which the doctor moved around awed them into silence.

"I'll need you both to place your hands firmly on the child's legs and arms, so he doesn't move about," he ordered the two of them.

"Child? Child, what is your name?" the doctor asked sweetly as I felt the hands of the nurse and wagon driver on the backs of my arms and legs.

"Piotr."

"Piotr, I am going to perform an operation on you. It will hurt quite a bit. But once it is all done, you'll begin to heal and feel much better. Do you understand me?"

I whimpered and nodded my head in understanding.

The doctor slowly strapped my legs down to the table as an extra measure against any abrupt movements. The nurse strapped down my arms then resumed her position holding them as well. The doctor proceeded to perform a rectal operation on me without the aid of any anesthetic. To this day, it is the most severe physical pain I have ever had to endure. I screamed the longest and loudest I have ever screamed in my life, and then I passed out. When I woke up I was back at the orphanage unable to move. I lay there nearly motionless for the next five days.

Matka came back for me soon after that. She came once again with papers, speaking severely to the staff. She took me into her arms and carried me outside. I was so happy to see her that I barely noticed Star in the wagon with us. Matka had once again saved us.

We rode along together, Matka holding on to me tightly on one side and Star huddled close on the other. We passed the same two villages I had passed on my way to the doctor several weeks earlier. I spotted the little shack where I had seen the mother and her son. No one was outside, but it didn't matter. I had my matka this time.

"Piotr, come here and lie on my lap," Matka said as we arrived at the train station. It was evening, and I was getting sleepy.

"Sleep, my child, and dream of knights and castles!" she whispered. I settled into my seat, snuggling in close to my matka who loved me.

As the train slowly pulled into Toruń hours later, the harsh jerk of the brakes aroused me from my sleep. I looked up and saw Matka smiling down at me.

"Piotr, I have a surprise for you," she whispered.

I had slept nearly the entire journey, but upon hearing that a surprise awaited me, I jolted awake.

"What is it?" I asked excitedly.

"Should I tell you now?" she asked.

She need not have asked. Of course, I wanted her to tell me. Surprises should never be kept secret.

"We don't live in the basement anymore. We live in the fortress tower!"

The fortress tower! Every boy dreams of living in a castle, and my dream had come true. How my matka managed to get a home in the tower was beyond what I could understand. I must have been the luckiest boy in Toruń.

As we stepped off the train, I was itching to get to our fortress tower. Matka reminded me that we had to take Star to that lady's house on the corner first. I begged Matka to bring Star home with us. I wanted her to see our new home, too, but Matka said that we couldn't. Reluctantly, I walked to the woman's house.

Our visit to Matka's friend's house wasn't as long as the first visit had been. The women chatted a bit before Matka told her that I was still ill and she wanted to be sure that I received enough rest.

"Was it worse than before?" the woman asked with concern.

I saw the tears well up in my matka's eyes as she responded.

"Far worse. These poor children have been through more than most of us, and in a much shorter time. If I could, I would kill the people who could do this. But where would that get me, and how would that help these children? We must play by their rules." Matka shook her head in disgust, while the other woman motioned for Star to sit on her lap.

Star snuggled up close to the woman, who caressed her head gently.

"At least they had each other," the woman said as her voice trailed off.

Matka nodded for me to go, so I got up and said goodbye to Star. Looking back, I wish I would have hugged her, kissed her, told her that I loved her and that she was my best friend always.

But I didn't. I was tired. I was happy to be with my matka. And I was excited about seeing our new home in the fortress tower.

Chapter 4

Life was good — I had Matka, I was feeling better, I was able to play with my friends, and I saw the gypsies. The gypsies arrived in Toruń every summer and always had something going on in their camp when they settled into town. There was music, dancing, singing, and — of course — trading. I had missed the majority of their visit to Toruń while I was recovering, but I was able to visit them once before they packed up their tents to begin their migration south.

Unfortunately, the fun didn't last for long.

Matka and I had spent the day wandering through town, visiting some of her friends. Most of the women had children, so we found ways to entertain ourselves as the adults conversed. Their talk was mostly food prices and idle gossip about other townspeople. When their voices became lower than a whisper, we knew they were either discussing us or the Soviet soldiers occupying our city. If a soldier had overheard some of their conversations, Matka and her friends would have been arrested and interrogated for weeks as spies. We constantly heard stories of innocent men and women being arrested for being spies. Out of the hundreds arrested, it was likely that only one was an actual spy, and the Soviets knew it. They hated us Poles, but we hated them more.

We went to bed early that night. It was cold, and I was tired. Matka snuggled into bed and drew me close. As she sang me a song,

I slowly drifted off to sleep, warmed by both her presence and her voice.

Screaming from the flats below us jolted me from my sleep. Men's voices boomed and echoed within the tower. Matka sat up next to me. She listened intently. We heard the sound of footsteps marching up the spiral stairs to our home at the top of the tower. Matka jumped out of bed and ran toward the door.

"Matka?" I asked, frightened.

She didn't have time to answer before we heard a deafening pounding on our door.

"Open up!" a man shouted.

Matka leaned hard against the door. Her lips were moving, but no sounds were coming out.

"Open up or we will force our way in!" the man shouted again.

"Matka!" I screamed in terror.

I watched as Matka slowly stepped away from the door. She wasn't about to open it, but she somehow knew that the man would push through. Within moments he had pounded his way into our room.

Standing in the doorway was one of the fiercest men I had ever seen. He was no more than twenty, but in his eyes brewed a rage well beyond his years. It seemed even he could not tell what he might do next, and that element of unpredictability only fueled his anger.

"Give me the child. We are leaving here immediately," he demanded as he made his way toward me.

Matka tried to remain calm.

"Where are we going?" she asked.

"WE are not going anywhere. I am taking this child, and you will stay put," he said, grabbing me out of bed.

I couldn't move. My body lay limp with fright. I couldn't scream out in terror, as I had done those other nights when the soldiers had come to take me to the orphanage. Tonight was different. Tonight I feared for my life.

"Get up, child, and move. Don't make me carry you." The soldier glared down at me with contempt.

Somehow I managed to put my two feet on the ground. My legs were shaking, and I could barely stand.

"Come, Piotr, let us put on some clothes," my matka said, maintaining a semblance of calm. She was trying to buy time, hoping the young soldier might be a little more lenient if he had a moment to calm his anger, a moment to remember we were human, just like him.

"No!" he yelled. "No clothes. Come, we're leaving now!"

I realized this was no ordinary collection of children. I wasn't going to be taken to the orphanage tonight. I could feel it. Matka felt it, too. She began begging the young man, pleading with him to tell her where he was planning to take me. He grabbed me and pushed passed my matka, ignoring her pleas.

I was dressed in a long nightgown that fell to my feet. My feet were bare. On my head I wore a cap Matka had made me earlier that autumn. I had been wearing it during the night, since the evenings had grown frigid. Winter was coming.

As we stepped out into the night air, I could feel the cold move straight through me. I tensed, curling my toes under my feet. The cold had taken the breath out of me, and I could hardly think of anything else for a moment. Then I saw my matka emerge from our tower. She wore nothing but a robe wrapped around her body. She was pursuing us. Seeing her in the distance caused me to remember my own situation, and I began kicking and screaming.

The soldier was unprepared for my outburst. I had been so quiet up to that point that he had temporarily forgotten I was even alive. My first kick landed right in the side of his stomach. He nearly dropped me in surprise.

He held me tighter in retaliation, forcing the air out of my lungs. I gulped for air and let out a scream. I could see Matka running faster, crying my name. No one came to our rescue. The townspeople must have heard us as we passed by their homes, but no one came outside to investigate. Everyone knew to mind their own business; otherwise, they might become victims, too.

We passed by the train station and headed left down a deserted road. Matka was gaining ground, because I had slowed the soldier. I was whimpering, but a loud popping sound soon silenced me. Matka stop in the middle of the road, frightened by the noise. A wave of recognition crossed her face, and she ran wildly toward us, yelling and screaming.

"No! Leave my child alone! NO!" she cried.

We turned the corner, leaving Matka still far off in the distance. I saw a small group of children, all crying and screaming. I immediately recognized them from my stay at the orphanage. Everyone around me faded into the background, however, when I noticed a large Mongolian soldier standing in the midst of the children.

This man was even more frightening than the soldier who had taken me from Matka. He was tall and burly, and his eyes were bloodshot. His face was dark with hatred, scowling at the crowd of children crying and screaming around him. As I stared at him, he picked up a young boy by the back of his neck. The boy was sobbing so hard that no sound could be heard from him, and snot ran down his face. With his free hand, the Mongolian forced a pistol inside the boy's mouth. He pulled the trigger without flinching. I watched as he carelessly threw the dead child onto a pile.

An intense fear struck me. I was here to die. We were all here to die.

I wet my pants.

I looked back at the pile where the Mongolian had thrown the little boy. Thick, dark, crimson blood oozed out of the pile of dead children. I was stunned. The soldier carrying me set me down amidst the group of frightened children waiting for their horrifying turns. I screamed and tried to grasp on to the soldier. He was evil and frightening, but he was better than the pile of corpses.

He pushed me aside and made his way over to a commanding officer, who sat near the road on his mount. My attention moved back to the Mongolian soldier who picked up the next child. I recognized her immediately. Her soft, dark brown hair swayed lightly against her back as he grabbed her by the arm. She was crying quietly. As he lifted her up, I screamed.

"No! Star! NO!" I yelled. My voice was hoarse and tears streamed down my face.

I watched in terror as the Mongolian lifted his pistol and shoved it hard into her mouth. She screamed. I saw her frightened blue eyes search the crowd for the voice she heard — for me — but before she could find me, the shot of the pistol rang through the air.

She was gone.

Star's head hung limply as the man tossed her onto the pile of dead children. She landed on top, blood running out of her mouth. Her eyes were still open, gazing blankly at me.

I died inside. The most innocent, beautiful person I had ever met had been slaughtered before my eyes. And why? Why did she deserve to die? What had she done to warrant such a horrible death? She was a child. She was just a little girl, raped too many times to count. She had done nothing to deserve the abuses she endured. And yet, they couldn't leave it at that.

I was beyond frightened. There was nothing I could do but stand there in the little group of children as, one by one, they were picked up and executed by the Mongolian. If I would have had the will to move, I might have tried to run away as fast as my small bare feet could take me. I no longer had the will. My best friend had died. The winter air, which had at one time been the cause of my shivering body, no longer affected me. Star's death had stunned me into frigid silence.

I knew my turn was coming, but I couldn't react. As the Mongolian soldier reached for me, I heard my matka. My matka! My senses heightened, and I searched the crowd of screaming children. I saw my matka approach the field and run straight to the commanding officer on the horse.

The Mongolian soldier picked me up. Suddenly, the fight in me returned. I didn't want to die. I didn't want to end up on that pile of children. I wanted to live — for Matka, for Star.

I wriggled as he grabbed me, but the Mongolian was too strong.

"Mamusiu!" I yelled. "Mamusiu!"

She didn't even turn my way. Instead, she ripped open her robe and bared her cold, naked body to the officer on the horse. The Mongolian shoved the end of the pistol into my mouth. It was warm and tasted of blood.

Before the Mongolian could pull the trigger, the commanding officer yelled for him to stop. The Mongolian sneered at me and threw me onto the pile of children.

I lay there stunned for a moment before realizing I was lying on a dead child. I immediately began coughing and gagging, trying to suppress the desire to throw up, as I found my way out of the pile of dead bodies. As I moved toward the bottom of the pile, I noticed Star only a few meters away, one arm outstretched in my direction. For an instant, I wanted to grab it, to hold it tightly. But I knew she was dead, and the thought made me sick. I wanted Matka.

The commanding officer rode toward me and lifted me off the pile of children and set me on the ground where Matka came running toward us. She stood nude before me but quickly covered herself with her robe and held me tight.

"Quickly, Piotr. We must leave this place."

We walked in silence. The commanding officer rode behind us, following us in the direction of our home. I was still shaking. The terror was not over yet. I wasn't safe. Why was the soldier coming with us? What would he do to us?

And then the thought of Star came crashing in on me; thinking of her lifeless eyes staring up at me from the pile made me shudder. Even today when I think of that night, I can clearly see her face and her eyes, wide with fright. I cry still. I cry like the lost child that I was. A child shouldn't see such things. A child shouldn't die that way.

As I thought of Star, Matka spoke to me, pulling me out of my trance.

"You will be okay, Piotrusiu. You will forget this day."

I nodded, hoping that could be true but knowing it would be impossible.

When we approached our home, Matka whispered something to the Soviet officer. He nodded and rode off. Then she took me by the hand and led me up the spiraling tower steps. I cried the whole way up the stairs, relieved the officer was gone but overwhelmed by the intensity of what I had just witnessed.

"Why, Matka, why?" I kept asking over and over.

She couldn't answer me. She was visibly shaking.

"You are safe, Piotrusiu. Matka is here. No one will harm you tonight. Matka won't let anyone hurt you."

She then carried me into bed and held me tight. She cried with me as I cried. She cried for Star. She cried for all the children. We cried until our bodies ached, and we could no longer cry another tear. Then we fell asleep.

The next morning the Soviet officer appeared outside our door. I was still sleepy; nightmares had kept me awake for most of the night. Matka invited him in, and he sat down at our small table. She dressed me in play clothes and made sure I was warm enough to go outside.

"You will go outside and play," she informed me. I knew this was not a question of whether I wanted to play, but a command that I must, even though I was afraid to leave her with the Soviet from the night before.

I didn't understand then why my matka would so kindly invite this Soviet into our home. I understand fully now. My matka had given herself in order to save me. Mothers are supposed to sacrifice for their children, but my matka went above and beyond. She sacrificed her body, allowing the Soviet soldier to use her, so that I could live. Is this what mothers do? Do they sell their bodies and their souls to protect their children? How many mothers would do that?

The soldiers that night didn't have sympathy for me; they didn't care whether I lived or died. They were simply following orders. A young, lonely commanding officer, however, had seen the terror in a beautiful woman's eyes. He had seen the artful curve of her body. He couldn't resist her desperate offer, not when he so longed for the warmth of a woman's touch. So my matka let him. She did this for me.

The soldier came to our house regularly after that. He usually brought food or some coal to warm our home. During those months, Matka would send me out to play, and I would come home to a warm house with delicious food on the table. Never once did we worry that I would be taken to the orphanages.

But the townspeople sneered at us. I heard some of the children repeat things they had heard their parents say about Matka and the Soviet officer. I felt ashamed that he visited us. We hated Soviets.

We despised Soviets. We didn't invite them into our home. But I also knew we were safe because of him. We never went cold or hungry. At that time, life was all about survival.

After months of relative security, the soldier arrived one morning with more food than I had ever seen in my entire life. Matka invited him in and at once began chopping up all of the vegetables he had brought, throwing them into the soup on the stove.

"I will be leaving tomorrow. I am going to be stationed in East Germany. I came to say goodbye," he said rather sadly.

Matka sat down heavily. I'm not sure if she was sad to see him go because she would miss him or if she was worried that his absence would once again bring about chaos for our lives. In either case, he never returned. And the chaos erupted once more.

Chapter 5

I stared into the mirror.

There is something about one's own reflection in a mirror that is slightly alarming. The reflection staring back at me was that of a frightened little boy. Physically I was thin, much too thin for a 7-year-old child. I had bruises on my arms and legs from the hard labor and frequent beatings I endured, but there weren't even enough of those to set me apart from any of the other orphans.

But a mirror doesn't tell the whole story. Behind that reflection were secrets left to be uncovered. What the mirror couldn't see, what it didn't reflect, was who I was. I was a lost boy. I missed my matka. I was scared. I was lonely. And more importantly, I knew I was not an orphan.

After the Soviet officer left us, I was sent to the orphanage yet again. This time, however, I was sent to an orphanage located in a small town outside of Bydgoszcz (bid-gosht), about 48 kilometers northwest of Toruń. The orphanage was large, much larger than the orphanage where I had stayed in Białochowo.

The building was made of glass; or at least, it seemed like it was. There were huge windows and expansive sliding glass doors all around the house. There were also mirrors everywhere. Every time I turned a corner, I found my frightened reflection staring back at me.

From time to time, I would stop and stare into the mirrors on my way to and from doing chores. As I stared into the eyes of that lost little boy, I would tell him he didn't belong there. I screamed that message inside my head every day that I woke up in the orphanage, but no one heard me.

Once I examined my face very closely. I leaned into the mirror as far as I could without touching it, taking note of my blue eyes and dark brown hair. They reminded me of Star. I was lonely in this orphanage without her. I missed her smile. I missed her friendship. I missed her most at night. I would lie in bed remembering how we used to sing songs that we had made up while working in the sugar beet fields. She would have snuggled up near me and told me everything would be okay when I missed my matka. No one here did that for me. My loneliness enveloped me, smothering me with complete emptiness. I needed my friend. I needed my matka. Thankfully, I didn't stay long.

There were several adults who managed the orphanage. Some took care that we were presentable by feeding us an appropriate amount of food or making sure we washed ourselves at least once a week. Other adults were there simply to supervise our work tasks, making sure we didn't slack on our jobs. One man in particular was quite brutal. He would beat children without any just cause. He seemed to find pleasure in inflicting pain.

One evening he decided he would do further damage. He grabbed me and a few other children, ordering us to follow him into a room upstairs. Once there, he began beating us mercilessly. We were seen as unwanted nuisances that deserved nothing more than a severe whipping. He left us there battered and bruised.

The second time he came around to beat us, I ran. We were upstairs, but I bolted past him and headed downstairs toward freedom. From the top of the stairs, I saw the light of an open door.

As I was running, I looked behind me to see if I was being chased, keeping one eye on the stairs below. I didn't need to run so fast if he had given up on me. But the man was right behind me, reaching out to grab a hold of me. I ran a little faster. It was just enough so that when he reached out he merely grabbed my shirt, providing me with enough room to wrench myself away from him. I ran as fast as my legs would take me down the straight steps.

I had forgotten that the house was made of glass. I had seen light and thought it was an open door to my freedom. I was sadly mistaken. I ran straight into the glass at full speed.

When I awoke I saw doctors in white jackets standing all around me. My head hurt so badly I could barely open my eyes. The blinding light accosted my brain like a serrated knife. I wanted to sleep. All I wanted to do was sleep.

When I awoke the second time, my matka stood over me, smiling. She had come to rescue me once again. Every time I was in too much pain to endure by myself, she somehow knew and managed to get me home to Toruń. In Toruń, I was safe with Matka for at least a few months before the Soviet soldiers came knocking again.

— — — — — — — — — — — — — — —

The gypsies came back into town shortly after Matka brought me home. Matka took me to see them almost every day. I never tired of visiting the gypsies. On previous visits to the gypsy camp, I had heard the long-winded stories about their travels. Those stories had imprinted themselves on my mind and now gave hope to my 8-year-old heart, hope that one day I, too, would become a gypsy. The gypsies had it all: travels, adventures, loot, and — most importantly — they were never alone. They were never tied down to one place, yet I knew they'd always come back to Toruń, bringing with them items to sell and trade from all over the world. If I were to join them, I'd be able to travel around the world and still come home and visit my matka.

When we arrived for our first visit to the camp that summer, the gypsy king was just emerging from his tent. He wore a long red robe, which fell down to his feet. His feet were bare, but he wore gold rings on his toes. There were all sorts of people milling about the camp. Some were gathering the items they hoped to trade the next day; others were playing a game with sticks. But they all stopped and turned to look as the king came out of his tent. He could never be missed; his presence was always felt. I grabbed hold of Matka's hand and pointed in the direction of the king. Her eyes crinkled at the sides, a smile forming on her face. She had seen him, and though we were in a crowd of people, he had seen us, too. The gypsy king smiled widely, though his long graying beard partially hid the corners of his mouth. Around his neck hung two thick gold chains, which clinked together as he made his way toward us.

"Piotr, my boy! You are certainly growing up tall," he observed happily. He lifted his large hand and patted me on the head, ruffling my hair.

"Julianna, you have raised a strong boy, I see. Is he home for good now?" he asked, turning to my matka as he pulled me close. I could smell the scent of pipe in his beard.

"For now. I'm still trying," she answered, meeting his eyes directly.

"Piotr is a strong boy. And you, Julianna, are a strong woman. You know my offer still stands?"

"If nothing else works, then it's the only option," she replied.

I had no idea what they were talking about, but I sensed the intensity and solemnity of their tone. Matka and the gypsy king were old friends who were always trying to make each other laugh. The serious tone seemed out of place. But it didn't last long, and soon the gypsy king knelt down before me.

"Would you like to be a gypsy one day, Piotr?"

I nearly cried. This was my dream.

"Please, can I?" I asked, excitement welling up within me.

He smiled and stood up. Turning to the crowd that had gathered, he declared, "When Piotr turns 14, he will inherit all my wealth. Piotr, you will be my son and become the king of the gypsies. You will have this whole tribe."

Then, with a sweeping gesture of his hand, he announced, "Behold, standing before you is your future king!"

The crowd began clapping and cheering, and then one by one they bowed their heads in my direction. I was in complete awe. For the very first time in my life I felt important. I felt like I was someone special. I looked up at Matka, who was beaming with pride.

As I stood there in complete surprise, both the adults and the children came to shake my hand and congratulate me on being chosen by the gypsy king. Not one of them seemed upset or surprised that

I would be a gypsy king one day. They accepted his declaration without a hint of displeasure or envy.

By the time I had shaken hands with the entire tribe, the sky had turned the light gray of dusk. As soon as the last rays of sunlight vanished, a fire was lit. The flames licked the night sky, and music began with the playing of instruments, singing, and dancing.

I was so captivated by the activity surrounding the fire that I hadn't noticed Matka and the gypsy king disappear. I looked around, wondering where they could have gone, but they were difficult to find in the large crowd. Before I could take a step to search them out, a young woman with long, shimmering brown hair grabbed me by the hand and led me closer to the fire.

The blaze of the fire soaked me in warmth. My face was aglow as I stared into the flames, mesmerized by the flickering light of orange, yellow, and red, which seemed to dance in rhythm with the music. Several women had already begun dancing, swaying their bodies to the music. Their skin glowed against the fire as beads of perspiration formed on their temples. They weren't hindered by the heat but instead slid smoothly into the harmonious ebb and flow of fire and music, warmth and rhythm.

A young boy, probably around my age, nudged me and caused me to tear my eyes away from the dancing women.

"Here's some food. Congratulations," he stated rather matter-of-factly, handing me a platter of ham and all kinds of vegetables.

"Thank you," I said politely, taking the platter.

I quickly sat down cross-legged and began chomping down the food. I hadn't realized how hungry I was. As I sat there eating, I wondered how the gypsies always had so much food. They were considered poor by the townspeople, who commented every summer on how the gypsies were in a caste well below them. Yet the gypsies always had food, while many of the townspeople went days without eating.

As I looked around, I counted seven wagons full of gypsy possessions. The gypsy king owned these wagons. I knew they were full of loot, as the gypsies were known to travel about the country, trading and stealing. I suddenly grasped the full meaning of the gypsy king's declaration to his people. I would be king, which meant that all of this would someday be mine. I would never go hungry again.

The idea of stealing frightened me, though. I had seen one too many boys get punished for stealing. But maybe I could order the other gypsies to do all the stealing. I would just be their leader.

As I sat in awe and wonder over my future inheritance, Matka and the gypsy king approached.

"Aha! Here is my prince. Are you enjoying the food?" the gypsy king bellowed.

I nodded, my mouth full.

"If you would really like to celebrate, then you must have a man's drink," he commanded as he motioned for a young, dark man to come toward him.

"Bring me the vodka."

The young man quickly ran inside a tent and brought out a large bottle of pale liquid.

"This will make you a man in no time," the gypsy king chuckled as he poured me a small glass.

"Careful, Piotr. Don't drink it too fast," my matka warned me as the gypsy king handed me the glass.

I was so excited to be included in the adult festivities that I ignored my matka's warning and gulped the liquid down in one sitting. My throat caught fire as the alcohol slid down into my stomach. My belly was instantly warmed. I gagged and clutched my throat, tears forming in my eyes. I had never tasted anything so strong and rancid in my life.

The gypsy king laughed heartily as I wiped the tears from my eyes. Matka laughed quietly, too.

"I told you to be careful!" she reproached me.

I decided I wouldn't drink any vodka for a very long time. I could wait many years before acquiring a taste for such adult delights. Maybe I would try it again on my fourteenth birthday when I was declared a man.

The rest of the night whirled by me in swaying hips, hypnotic music, and the glow of the warm fire. I don't remember walking home that night, but the next morning I awoke in the excitement of knowing that my dreams of being a gypsy would one day become a reality.

————————————————

We visited the gypsies nearly every day that summer — trading goods, swapping stories, and celebrating together through song, dance, and bonfires. But on one of those summer days, my visit to the camp brought me a new friend who was not a gypsy.

Matka had gone off to speak with the gypsy king privately, leaving me to explore the gypsy campsite. It was the heat of the day, and most of the gypsies were off trying to trade in town. Those who remained at the camp were either very old or sleeping off the previous night's celebrations. The camp was quiet. I played with the puppies that roamed around the campsite, but eventually they became tired of fetching and left me to find some shade where they curled up and slept.

I wasn't tired. I had slept well the night before, dreaming of castles and kings. I looked around me at the deserted camp and decided that I needed more thrill and adventure, so I made my way toward my old stomping grounds. I wanted to see if I would finally be able to make it up the fortress wall. Now that I was older and had grown several inches, I thought I might have a chance of conquering it and declaring it mine. The wall wasn't too far from the camp, so I knew Matka would be able to find me without too much effort.

As I made my way to the wall, I passed under some trees and became distracted by a large stick on the ground, which resembled a medieval sword I had once seen in a picture book Matka had shown me.

"Aha!" I yelled to myself, since there wasn't a soul around.

I had found a perfect sword to take back to my tower window. Now I could be a real soldier, alerting Matka if a Soviet soldier were to stop by unannounced. Maybe this time we would have a chance of escaping before they tried to take me away again.

I struck a rock with the large stick, making sure my new sword wouldn't crack under the pressure. I wanted it to be sturdy, in case I came upon some enemies. The stick remained intact and made a soft, dark mark on the spot where it had struck the rock. I was pleased.

After examining my new sword for some time, I raised my head, sensing that someone was watching me. I wouldn't call what I felt fear, but rather a moment of uneasiness. I slowly turned around and noticed a boy off in the distance. I had been so involved in my discovery that I hadn't noticed him approach. While I was striking the rock, he had taken a seat on the ground near some bushes. He sat very still, watching my every movement. From afar I didn't recognize him. The boy looked about my age, though, so I felt a little more at ease.

"Do you like my new sword?" I bellowed over to him.

He didn't respond. He sat where he was, still barely moving.

"Hey, you! Do you like this stick I found?" I tried again.

The boy moved his head, looked behind him, and then seemed to realize that I was talking to him. For a moment he looked surprised that I would try to converse with him.

"Um…yeah. I like it," he finally responded, but I could barely hear him. I got the feeling he didn't wish to bring any unnecessary attention to himself.

I marched over to where the boy sat. If he liked it, then I might as well show him the sword up close. I wanted him to see the natural, sphere-like shape it had at the top of the stick; I wanted him to realize how much it resembled a true sword.

The boy cowered as I approached. He sat on his bottom with his feet pulled into his body, his face buried in his knees.

"This is my sword," I declared. All I could see were his two dark brown eyes gazing up at me just over the tops of his knees, but something about them looked strange.

I held out my sword for him to take, but he kept his face behind his knees.

"My name is Piotr. What's yours?" I asked politely.

"Dieter."

"Don't you want to check out my sword, Dieter?" I asked, but he didn't respond. "Why are you hiding your face?"

Slowly, Dieter lifted his head from his knees. As he faced me, I understood. His face was horrific. He was by far the most hideous-looking person I had ever laid eyes on. His face looked like it had been bashed in with my large stick. If you have ever had a baby doll and pushed its nose in, you might have an idea of how this poor young boy looked. And yet his eyes, which weren't even level since one seemed to slide down his face, were the kindest eyes I had ever seen. They seemed even kinder than those of my matka. He reminded me of one of the puppies I had played with earlier — so innocent and yet so wary.

I stared. I couldn't help but stare. Dieter never met the gaze of my eyes; he just kept looking down. I gathered myself in enough time to ask:

"So, Dieter, do you want to see my sword or not?"

Dieter looked at the sword and then at me. For a moment it seemed he couldn't decide whether he should trust me. I'm not sure what he expected I would do. Perhaps he thought I would beat him with the stick, because he flinched when I extended it in his direction. Looking back, I believe most people either cried in horror or simply laughed at him when first seeing him.

I won't lie — I was horrified by his appearance. But he was a boy just like me. I understood what it meant to be abused and laughed at. I knew I didn't like it. And I was sure he had experienced similar abuses in his life. Plus, I liked him. Maybe it was because he seemed worse off than me. Maybe it was the way he looked at me with longing in his eyes for a friend.

In either case, I extended my sword to him. He took it and smiled. It was the most beautiful smile I had ever seen. It wasn't physically beautiful; in fact, it was slightly scrunched into more of a sidewise slant. But it was genuine. Never again have I seen a smile as genuine and grateful as his.

That afternoon we played together as though we had been friends forever. As the sun shifted behind some clouds, eventually disappearing into the night sky, I decided I ought to find my matka. I promised Dieter we would continue our game of knights and kings the following afternoon.

— — — — — — — — — — — — — — —

Dieter and I spent the rest of that summer playing together. We would walk about town, peering into shop windows, racing each other down the cobblestone streets, or climbing brick walls and large trees. Matka always told me to come back at dark, but Dieter and I always found some excuse to stay out a little later.

Matka loved Dieter instantly. She didn't flinch or even hesitate as I had done when I first met him. Instead, she smiled her beautiful smile at him as though he were just a regular boy like my other friends. And just like when she met the other boys, she offered Dieter food and told him that he needed to fatten up. She asked him who his family was and where he was staying. When he told her that he had no family, but that he was staying with a lady in town, Matka grabbed him by the shoulders and pulled him toward her. She gave him an enormous hug and told him that she and I were special people to have found a new friend in him. Dieter smiled like a man that evening.

I loved Dieter, too. Sometimes when we went into town together, shopkeepers would stare or yell out obscenities at him. I discovered an anger I had never felt before. All I wanted to do was protect him from the ignorant eyes of those who were insensitive to the obvious abuses he endured. I wasn't able to protect Star, but I was bigger and stronger now. If someone wanted to mess with Dieter, they were going to have to mess with me, too. In my mind, Dieter was my brother, and no one would hurt him and get away with it. I was smart, though, because I understood that sometimes the best forms of revenge were the ones carried out much later, when the perpetrator was unprepared.

I remembered the face of every person who had caused Dieter to wipe away tears of hurt. I remembered them all, and they were going to feel my wrath. No one had the right to hurt this boy. No one.

— — — — — — — — — — — — — —

But that summer with Dieter, like all good things in my life, came to an end when I was sent back to another orphanage. By that time I was almost getting used to the Soviet soldiers knocking on our door. Matka would plead and beg, but they always refused to listen.

Then she would lean over, give me a kiss, and tell me that she would come and get me soon. I knew Matka would keep her promise, but I still feared the abuses that would come before she arrived.

The new orphanage was located outside of Chełmno (helm-no), approximately 45 kilometers north of Toruń. I saw several kids I knew from previous stays. I was happiest, however, when I realized that Dieter had been taken to the orphanage with me. We had a pretty rough time with the other kids during our first week, but we stuck together. No one liked Dieter because of the way he looked, but that wasn't going to stop me from being his friend. I understood what it meant to be a true friend, so there was no way I would back down —despite the harsh words they threw at me as well.

On one particular day, we were outside fulfilling one of our menial chores when I heard a voice call out from behind us. I turned, but the boy looked mean and unruly. I turned back around and kept walking. The last thing I wanted was to meet this kid face-to-face. He looked like someone who might spit in my eye.

"Hey, you!" he yelled again, this time making his way toward me and Dieter as we followed some of the other children out into the fields to work.

Again, we ignored him.

"Listen, ugly! I'm talking to you."

Something deep within me snapped. I knew he wasn't talking to me. I had heard others call Dieter ugly, but something about the insolence of this boy made me boil in anger. I could feel my face get hot. I looked down at my hands and found them already balled tight into fists.

Dieter kept walking. He had grown accustomed to people yelling at him. He didn't notice that I had stopped walking beside him. He was just intent on ignoring the boy.

"You're ugly, too, but I'm talking to that guy," the kid said to me. "Yeah, you — ugly! Your mother must have been the ugliest whore ever born!"

Some other boys had gathered around by that time and began laughing uncontrollably at the insult. I turned to look at Dieter. His shoulders slouched, and I knew he had taken the comment to heart. He didn't know his mother. He had never met her, because she died in the war. But he loved her. I knew that if he weren't crying now, he would be later.

I turned back around to the boys. There were four of them, and I counted each one before I took a step toward them. I was tired of people picking on Dieter just because he was an easy target. If they wanted to pick on someone, they should pick on me.

My fists were still clenched as I approached them. I didn't say a word.

"Who do you think you are? Ugly's guardian angel? Huh? Why do you want to hang around him? You might get his disease! You want to look like that, too, or something?" the kid taunted as I slowly made my way toward him.

My anger was controlled. I was just waiting for the right moment.

The group of boys saw that I was approaching, but they didn't seem to care. They saw the clenched fists heading their way, but they kept throwing out insult after insult. When I was just a few meters away from them, I stopped.

"What? You have a problem?" asked the leader.

I didn't answer.

Instead, I ran into them at full speed, knocking the leader of the pack straight to the ground. I sat on top of him, swinging and punching with all my might. I hit him in the stomach. I hit him in the face. I heard him crying, but I didn't care.

"You deserve this," I yelled. "You asked for this!"

I didn't realize that the other three boys had started punching and kicking me. My body felt the pain, but my mind was on the task at hand. This kid needed to feel the pain that Dieter felt every time someone called him a name or pointed out that he looked different.

"Piotr, stop!" yelled Dieter from a distance. He had realized that I wasn't at his side anymore.

"Piotr! They're killing you!" he yelled.

Hearing his voice made me realize that I was no longer on top of the leader. He was still lying on the ground a few meters away, but I was also on the ground, with three boys punching and scratching at me. In defense, I kicked one right in the chin, knocking him to the ground, where he remained. The other two only punched me harder, so I flailed trying to protect myself.

Three adults came running toward us from the fields. They pried the two boys off me, yelling at us the entire time.

"What do you think you're doing?" the woman screamed as the two men held each of the boys still standing.

"Who started this?" they asked.

The boys pointed at me.

"Look, he knocked both of them out!" cried the smaller of the two boys.

The adults had already noticed the other two boys lying motionless on the ground. They never asked why the fight had started. They picked me up and forced me to walk back into the fields.

"You will work without dinner or breakfast!" the woman screeched as she watched me hobble into the fields.

My arms and legs ached. Blood was dripping from my head, but they didn't seem to care that I was hurt. All I was to them was a troublemaker, plain and simple. And a troublemaker always needs punishing.

I passed by Dieter as I entered the fields.

"Thank you," he whispered.

I smiled at him. His thanks was all I needed to hear to work the fields with an extra fervor. No one would stop me. Not ever.

Chapter 6

"What did you say?" I demanded as I whirled around, my fists tightening for action.

The boy facing me looked scared.

"I-I-I just said…um…that the dog over there is ugly," he stammered as he pointed to a lazy dog lying in some shade on the side of the orphanage. The other kids around him slipped away as he tried to explain.

"I had a dog by my house that was much better than that lousy dog. That dog over there just eats and lies around. I hate him, is what I said. I'm sorry. Is he your dog?"

My body relaxed a bit as I realized the boy hadn't directed his comment toward Dieter. After only a few months in the orphanage outside of Chełmno, I had already wound up in several fights. My anger boiled every time someone insulted Dieter. I wanted to fight until the insults stopped forever. But I was only 9 years old, and the continuous fighting made me tired, physically and emotionally drained.

"Sorry if he's your dog. It's just that he's dumb. My dog was much smarter," the kid said, still explaining.

"No, he's not my dog. I thought you said something else," I answered, slowly turning back to Dieter, who had already gone on to the fields.

For a moment I thought about running to catch up to him, but I was exhausted. I hadn't slept much in the past few months. I kept having nightmares about Matka. I would wake up trembling and hoping that she was all right. Plus, all the work we had to do in the fields was taking a toll on my body. I was tired of picking all day long. And I was tired of getting into fights.

"Oh. Well, do you have a dog? Because I don't really have a dog. I call it mine, because it hangs out by my house. I give it bread once in awhile. My dad is a baker. He makes delicious bread. Better than this bread here."

The boy kept talking to me even though my back was to him. At the mention of his father, I snapped. Normally I wouldn't have reacted so strongly, but I think the lack of sleep was getting the best of me.

"If you have a dad, how come you're here?" I shot at him, ignoring the question about the dog.

The boy stood there for a moment in silence. I knew my words had hurt him more than any punch to the face could have. I immediately felt remorse. Here I was trying to protect Dieter from insults and harsh words, yet I had managed to hit this kid's weak spot.

"It's alright. I have a mother and I'm here, too," I said, feeling bad for the way I had snapped at him. "I don't know why they keep bringing me here. I can't understand why they won't leave me and Matka alone."

The boy relaxed a little, but his face still held the pain of my comment.

"I don't know why, either. I think I know why, but I don't like talking about it. My dad always tells the Soviet soldiers to leave us alone — that he loves me no matter what — but they don't listen. They never listen," he explained quietly, looking down at his hands.

For the first time since our conversation began, I really looked at him. He was much darker than the rest of us children. His tan seemed almost too dark and even. He had blue eyes, but they were much narrower than my own. He was taller than me by an inch or two, but just as thin.

Years later I learned that his mother had been raped by one of the German officers stationed in Toruń during the war. He was the product of that one night of terror. Since his birth father was an unknown German soldier of Turkish descent, the Soviet officers felt it their duty to ship him off to the orphanages with the rest of us, despite the fact that both his mother and stepfather loved him and wanted him.

"I know what you mean. I hate the Soviets," I replied.

"Me too," he said. He looked at me for a moment, obviously sizing me up. The creases above his eyes furrowed, as though he were deep in thought.

"What's your name?" he asked, startling me a bit. I had half expected him to punch me from the way he was looking at me.

"Piotr," I answered, unsure where the conversation might be leading.

"Mine is Henryk," he proclaimed proudly. He held out his hand for me to shake.

I smiled, understanding that he had forgiven me for my comment about his father. As I shook his hand, I knew that we would be friends for a long time. He and I were alike. We both had parents who loved us, yet we were still considered orphans.

I looked around and noticed that Henryk and I were standing in the fields. We had walked there while we were talking, and I hadn't even realized it.

We chose a row of sugar beets in the center of the fields. Henryk began picking immediately, setting his basket down beside him. I hesitated for a moment as I looked down the row. In the distance I could see Dieter already picking away. He looked intent, obviously concentrating on the task at hand. I, however, was in no mood to be picking. My arms ached from the day before. The sun, still high in the sky, beat down on me, causing me to feel woozy. I hated picking.

There were more important things I could be doing with my time. Instead of picking, I could be talking with Matka about my fights. She said she didn't like fights, but I never did believe her. She seemed to enjoy my stories too much to disapprove. Her eyes would grow bright and alert whenever I told her how I stuck up for myself or for Dieter. She would say, "Now, Piotr, if you can stay out of a fight, you should." But then she would lean toward me and kiss me on the forehead, so I knew she was proud.

Sometimes when I would tell her I got into a fight, she wouldn't reproach me at all, but instead insisted on all the details. She would first ask why I got into a fight. When I told her that someone was picking on Dieter, she would smile and tell me she loved me. Then she would ask me when it was that I threw my first punch and where I ended up hitting my target. She wanted to picture the scene in her head.

She always ended by asking me what Dieter did. Sometimes I would tell her about how he was brought into the fight and threw his own punches, and other times I would tell her how he stayed out of it. She would smile to herself and say, "Dieter is a smart boy. He's lucky to have a friend like you, but you are even luckier to have him as your friend. Remember that." Then she would pat me on the head and tell me to get to bed.

I smiled to myself as I thought of Matka. I missed her so much, but at least this orphanage was better than the last one. We were beaten on occasion, but for the most part they left us alone in the fields. Plus, I had a friend with me, which made missing Matka much easier.

"You ever miss your mother so much you ache inside?" Henryk asked me out of the blue. We had been working alongside each other in silence for quite some time.

"Yes. I was just thinking of her."

"Me too. My mother is beautiful," he said, smiling.

"Mine too."

Henryk and I picked side by side until dusk. I lost track of Dieter, but I was pretty sure he was picking away like the rest of us. Dieter was one hard worker. I could barely keep up with him when he picked in the fields. The adults couldn't treat him as poorly when he brought in a heavy load at the end of every working day.

I worked hard too, but my heart wasn't in it. I didn't care what the adults thought of me. Some of them were kind, but they were the women who would volunteer their time on Saturdays to give the other adults a day off. The regular adult attendants could be brutally severe.

"I'm just about sick of this, aren't you?" Henryk asked as he chuckled to himself.

"I've been sick of this since the first day! What I want to do right now is take a swim in the Wisła River. And then after that, eat Matka's warm, delicious soup," I said dreamily.

"Yeah. And eat some of my dad's fresh-out-of-the-oven bread. And after that, I would go into town and try to climb the brick wall by the sewer."

"Oh, man. I've been trying to climb the brick wall by my house for years. I still haven't got to the top yet. I was going to try one day when I was out by the gypsy camp, but I never got around to it. Then I was taken here."

"Oh, the gypsies come to your town, too?" Henryk asked.

"Yeah. I know the gypsy king. He gave me vodka and told me I was going to be the king of the gypsies," I boasted.

"You lie. The gypsies don't really like townspeople!" he laughed, as he swung a stalk in my direction, "You, the gypsy king. Now that is funny!"

"It's true. One day I'll prove it to you," I told him, not really worried that he didn't believe my story. I knew the truth, which was all that mattered.

"I would like that. I want to meet the gypsy king, actually. He has a lot of loot."

"And that loot is going to be mine someday!"

"Then I better be your friend, so you can give me some of your loot. Then I'll sell it back to the townspeople the gypsies stole it from and make lots of money!"

"You bet." I picked up my basket, which was getting quite heavy. "Where are you from, anyway?"

Henryk bent down to pick his basket up as well. The sun was setting, causing the sky to burst into bright colors of orange and pink. All around us children were picking up their baskets and making their way back toward the orphanage to give the adults their product.

"Toruń."

"Me too!"

"Then I will meet the gypsies when we get back!" he laughed.

"I guarantee it."

— — — — — — — — — — — — — — — —

One Saturday while most of the regular adult attendants went into town for their day off, the volunteers decided to give us a treat — a trip to watch a movie in Chełmno, the town a couple of kilometers from the orphanage. I sat in the middle of the wagon with Dieter on one side of me and Henryk on the other. We were so excited about seeing a film we could hardly sit still. I had seen a movie in the first orphanage where I stayed, but that seemed so long ago.

"I've never seen a film before," Dieter said as we rode into town.

"You'll like it. It's almost like you're part of the movie," I said excitedly.

"Is it scary?"

"No, it's exciting! You get to go to lands you've never seen before."

Dieter smiled, rubbing his hands together.

Several children had asked what movie we were going to see, but the adults only told us it was going to be about cowboys and Indians.

"Is there fighting?" asked Henryk.

The young, pretty volunteer nodded her head and smiled.

"Yes, there is fighting for the little boys and some romance for the little girls."

We snickered at the romance part. Who would want to see that? But then I thought of Star. Maybe she would have wanted to see some romance.

"Okay, we're here. Everybody out and into single-file lines," the older woman yelled at us as we piled out of the wagon.

Dieter grabbed the back of my shirt as we headed into the dark theatre. The movie had already started, so we were directed toward the back rows. We sat behind another group of orphans, who were much more neatly dressed, but I wasn't concerned about them. We were seeing a film.

Before us was a huge screen, much larger than the one I had seen at the Białochowo orphanage. The screen showed two men wearing tall, rounded cowboy hats and sitting on long-legged horses, talking in a language we had never heard before. I didn't know what they were saying, but on the bottom of the screen there were some words that I could barely read. My matka had taught me to read a little bit, but the words flashed so fast that I missed much of what was going on.

"What's happening?" Dieter whispered.

"The cowboys are going to go fight the Indians, I think."

We sat in hard folding chairs, which made my bottom numb if I didn't move every once in awhile. I hardly noticed, though. The film was gripping. I didn't catch most of what was going on, but I knew that the good guys were the cowboys. I wanted to be a cowboy, too.

The cowboys lived in a huge, desert-like land. The land looked so vast and free. And they could ride their horses wherever they wanted to go. America! Now that was a place I could see myself living. I would wear a large cowboy hat and have a long-legged brown horse to ride from town to town.

As I daydreamed about being one of the cowboys, the story took a turn for the worse. The cowboys were no longer winning their wars. The Indians were fighting back with all their might. Out of their teepees they flew with bows and arrows. Their teepees and bonfires reminded me of the gypsy camp a little bit. The chief of the Indians was nothing like the gypsy king, though. The Indian chief was tall and thin and wore paint on his face like a warrior. My gypsy king was too jolly to look so severe.

Soon the Indians caught up with a couple of cowboys who had separated from the main group. One of the cowboys was shot with a bow and arrow right through the heart. He fell forward onto his horse, gripping the arrow tightly, before he toppled over dead. Dieter gasped as he sat on the edge of his seat.

The Indians managed to corner the remaining cowboy. We expected him to be shot, too, but for some reason the Indians decided to try to talk to him instead. The cowboy pulled out his gun, shot one of the Indians, and rode away to safety.

As he reached the town, other cowboys had already gathered together in a saloon where they were drinking and playing card games. Then a dark, shaggy man wearing all black came into the saloon. The theatre grew quiet as he stepped to the bar to order a drink. We knew this was a bad guy.

All of a sudden a fight broke out. Cowboys were attacking other cowboys. Tables and chairs were moved out of the way as the bartender cowered behind his bar. Henryk stood up, cheering on the fight. Some of the other boys had stood up as well. The adults whispered loudly at us to sit down and watch from our seats, but the excitement was so intense. I even heard one little girl softly crying to herself.

Then the dark cowboy shot someone in the back, and the fight stopped. The tall, dark figure stood straight in the midst of the chaos around him and then ran out of the bar and jumped onto his horse. He rode off into the sunset, a fugitive.

The rest of the movie became a blur of cowboys searching for the tall, dark man while fighting off Indians. Toward the end of the movie, they caught the fugitive and had him stand on a platform attached to a tree. The sheriff placed a rope around the man's neck and kicked the platform away from the tree. The man hung limply, slowly being strangled to death. His body swung back and forth as we silently watched in horror. While the scene before us terrified most of the other children, I couldn't help but think that at least the fugitive wasn't being chased anymore. At least he was at peace.

The movie ended on a happy note. The hero married the beautiful girl, and they had a wedding, which made all the little girls very happy. My thoughts were with the hanging fugitive, though. He had been my hero.

Chapter 7

A few weeks after Matka rescued me from the Chełmno orphanage, her brother returned to Toruń. He had been stationed elsewhere in Poland but was back home on leave. Franek Szczepański was a tall man, thin and noble looking. Whenever I saw him, which wasn't often given the Polish army's tendency to station him somewhere other than Toruń, he wore his brownish green Polish uniform — always pressed to perfection.

Sometimes Franek would bring his wife along on his visits to our house. She was a very pretty woman, but she always seemed sad. Her eyes were large and brown, and she pulled her hair up in a tight bun behind her head.

I once asked Matka why my auntie always looked so sad. For once Matka didn't answer me in vague terms. She explained that Uncle Franek had been hurt in the war, so he could never have children. My auntie loved Franek; she would never leave him. But that meant she could never have children of her own.

I felt sorry for my auntie, because she seemed like she would be a good mother. She always brought me goodies when she came to visit, and she would sit beside me and pat my head. Though I barely knew her, I loved her because I knew she had endured pain. If nothing else, I could understand suffering.

Franek didn't arrive with his wife for this particular visit. Instead, he arrived with a grave look on his face. Matka let him in immediately, motioning him to sit down.

"The police will be coming for Piotr again," he began. "They're rounding up children in all the surrounding towns. They've cleared out all the German and Jewish orphans just north of us in Chełmza and Świecie."

In recent months, the Soviets had begun to delegate duties to the Polish police in order to conserve Soviet manpower. The police were pleased to be given the added responsibility. The menial tasks they had been carrying out over the last ten years had left them feeling defeated. They were ready and eager to carry out more meaningful tasks, even if the orders came from the Soviets.

Matka sat down at the table next to her brother. Her face looked drawn and tired.

"What can I do?" she asked, almost in a whisper.

"There's nothing you can do to stop them from taking him away. We can't hide him. They will find him, as they always do."

"Why won't they just leave these children alone? If they are wanted, then what is the difference? Then they don't have to feed them and take care of them!"

I sat in the corner of our tower room, listening to their conversation. I didn't want the police to come for me. I had barely been home three weeks from the last orphanage. I had hardly spent any time with Matka at all. Plus, the gypsies hadn't returned to town, so I hadn't introduced them to Henryk. There was so much I wanted to do that would be ruined if the police were to come and take me away again.

"Julianna, listen. They keep taking him because you have no legal right to him. We need to get these adoption papers approved so that he no longer has to go to the orphanage. I will be on leave for two months. Rather than have the police come for him, let's take him to a Catholic orphanage. They will treat him better. Together you and I will get the right documents, so he never has to be taken to another orphanage again!"

Uncle Franek pounded on the table loudly. "We will be free of their meddling into our affairs. You want this child, Julianna, then we will get you this child!" he proclaimed.

Matka lowered her head, her eyes staring down at the table.

"I can't stand to see him sent off, but if there is a chance that this may be the last time, then we will do it."

"You're making the right decision. And he will be safe with the Catholics."

Franek handed Matka some papers, and the two discussed their plan in greater detail. It was getting late, so I crawled into bed. I had heard that I was going to be sent to the orphanages again, which made me uneasy. I didn't see how any orphanage could be good. If they didn't beat me or abuse me, then they worked me like an animal. I just wanted to be a child. But Matka seemed to agree to Franek's suggestion when he mentioned the adoption papers. I didn't understand what the adults meant by adoption papers. But if it allowed my matka to keep me out of the orphanages for good, then I would be all for them. If there was anyone I could trust, it was Matka. She never failed me.

The next morning Matka woke me up very early.

"Hurry, Piotr. *Wujek* Franek will be here any moment."

My eyes felt heavy with sleep.

"We will be taking you to a safe orphanage before the police come to take you away to a bad one. This way you will be safe until we have everything sorted out."

This news had me fully awake. I didn't want to go to an orphanage. I didn't realize we would have to go so soon.

"Mamusiu, I don't want to go!" I cried.

"Piotrusiu, I know, but it's for the best," she tried to assure me.

I curled up into the fetal position, holding my knees tightly to my chest and burying my head in my arms.

"Come, Piotr. I know you don't want to go. But I talked to the *pani* taking care of Dieter, so he too will be at this orphanage. It will be safer for you both, because the police are coming soon and will take you to a bad place. Believe me, Piotr, when I say that this is for the best. I don't want you to go either, but it's something that must be done so that you never have to go again."

She lay down beside me, wrapping her arms around my little body. She kissed the back of my head.

"Come, Piotr, let Mamusia hold you."

I let go of my knees and slowly turned myself around to face her. She grabbed me and pulled me in tight, so I felt the warmth of her body. She squeezed me, and I held her back. We lay like this, holding one another as though we might never see each other again, until Franek came.

— — — — — — — — — — — — — — — —

We arrived in Grudziądz in the middle of the afternoon. We stepped off the train and into the bustling town. I remembered the town from the first time I had been taken to an orphanage. To the right of the train platform I saw wagons sitting, waiting for customers who needed a ride to the outskirts of town. The wagons reminded me of my first trip to Białochowo. It was there I had first met Star.

"We can walk to the orphanage from here," Franek told us as he led us toward the main street.

The town of Grudziądz was decently sized, but not as nice as Toruń. Off the main street there were tall buildings made of brick, but I could make out no fortress walls or any defining characteristic of Poland's medieval past. I didn't like the place already.

Matka walked beside me, holding my hand as we moved out of the town and into the countryside. There were tall trees dotting the landscape as we made our way down a straight road.

"Dieter will be here, too?" I asked, making sure I had heard Matka right earlier.

"He will be coming soon."

I knew I was supposed to feel some sort of relief in knowing that my friend would be with me, but I didn't. I was still frightened by what I might endure during my stay.

After some time, we arrived at a large building off to the left of the road. It was a dark building, with what looked like a chapel sitting neatly on the adjacent lot. Behind the building I could see gravestones rising up from the ground.

"This is the Catholic orphanage I told you about. I've heard they treat the children here very well," Franek said as we made our way up the walk.

A stern woman in black greeted us at the door. She stared down at us from the front steps as we approached. Upon seeing Franek in his Polish uniform, her face brightened.

"Welcome, sir! Thank you so much for what you do for us in the service. We know you are God's soldiers sent to protect us!" she proclaimed loudly. I thought she might wake up the dead.

Franek simply bowed in her honor. I huddled closer to Matka.

"Why is she wearing that black robe and that hood?" I whispered.

"She's a nun. That is the dress that all nuns wear," Matka explained.

It looked pretty silly to me.

"We are dropping off this boy. He is an orphan, and we ask that you please take care of him until we get the proper paperwork ready for my sister here to adopt him legally. Here is his paperwork," Franek stated abruptly as he handed the nun some papers.

"We will do so happily." She smiled weakly as she glanced over the paperwork.

Franek turned to me and extended his hand for me to shake. Then he knelt to my level and told me, "You be a soldier, Piotr. We will get things straightened out and come for you soon. Until then, be strong and courageous."

Then he patted me softly on the back and turned for the gate. Matka reached down and hugged me tightly.

"I will think about you every day until we come for you. You will be here in my heart, and I will be in yours, right?"

I nodded in agreement, tears streaming down my face.

"You will be brave, Piotr. And in no time, I will be back for you, and you will never have to go to another orphanage again! Think about that! Just remember that I love you."

Then she hugged me again and kissed me lightly on the cheek.

"I love you, too, Mamusiu," I whispered to her.

She smiled at me, stood up, and faced the nun.

"I'm trusting you to take care of him. He is all I live for."

The nun stared blankly at her. Then Matka swiftly turned around and followed Franek out the gate. I watched as they made their way down the street together. I could barely see their figures in the distance when the nun tugged at my shirt from behind.

"Come inside, child. You won't be seeing them for a long time."

I grudgingly followed the nun up the front steps and into the entrance of my new home. There wasn't a soul in sight. I could hear no voices of children in the upstairs rooms or even on the property grounds. All that could be heard was silence.

I stood in the middle of the foyer, my eyes wide with curiosity. My back was turned to the nun as I glanced at the room around me, taking in my new surroundings.

I was surprised at how quiet it was. Where could everyone be? All of the other orphanages I had been sent to were loud and boisterous with the constant movement of children. I couldn't get past how eerily tranquil this particular orphanage was in comparison to the others.

The silence was broken in a flash.

"You *Niemiec* child!" screeched the nun from behind me, her voice echoing off the walls of the foyer where we stood.

Frightened, I quickly swirled around to face her. She stood before me, holding the papers Franek had handed her. Her eyes glared at me like those of the Soviet soldier I had seen the night Star had been murdered. Then, without warning, she came at me and bashed me over the head with something long and hard.

My head reeled as I fell to the floor in shock. Pain seared down my neck, causing a massive headache. I stared up at the woman standing over me, unsure if she had really caused me such pain. After all, she was a small woman, barely 5 centimeters taller than me.

"We will find your father, and he will pay for the lives he took away! And you will pay for the sins of your father!" she screamed at me again.

I had no clue what she was talking about. My mind jumped all over the place as I tried to figure out what I had done. All I kept hearing her chant was *twoj ojciec* over and over again. I was truly confused, because I didn't even think I had a father. In fact, I had never even wondered why I didn't have one. I never asked Matka where he was. I just assumed one never existed.

I lay still on the floor, not wanting to move. All I could feel was the pain at the top of my head. I reached up and touched it, immediately tensing in agony. The point where she had hit me was quite tender. I cried softly to myself, thinking how wrong Franek had been about this place being a safe orphanage. After all, I had already been hit over the head, and I hadn't even been here an hour.

The nun kept rambling on and on about "German scum" she had encountered during the war. As I lay there holding my head, she walked around me explaining how she wished she could make every German pay for the death and destruction her hometown had endured. I realized she wasn't really talking to me; she was just unleashing a torrent of passion she had probably kept bottled up for years. She was clearly crazy, and I wanted nothing to do with her.

As she spoke of the terrors of the war, she became animated. Her pace quickened as she circled around me like a predator ready to pounce on his prey. She expressed herself with hand motions, sometimes slapping her thigh loudly, as she thought of something immeasurably horrible the Germans had done to someone she knew. At one point she switched directions, circling me counterclockwise. In doing so, she stepped rather close to my head, causing me to clutch it tighter in defense. I wasn't sure what this small, angry woman was capable of.

My sudden movement caused her to pause in her speech. For the first time, I think she fully realized that I was present for her temper tantrum. She stood over me for what seemed an eternity.

"Get up, child. I will show you something." Her voice was cold and emotionless, nothing like the emotional fervor she had expressed just moments before.

Something about the frigidness of her voice caused me to sit upright immediately. Her hot and cold emotions frightened me. She was an unstable woman, and I was at her disposal. And there was no one around to protect me.

"Follow me," she said as she turned abruptly toward a doorway leading into another room.

Reluctantly I rose from my position on the floor. My head swam as I stood for the first time since being hit. The room swirled around me, making me ill. My head pounded.

"Don't stand there, boy. Come," she demanded.

I took a few steps toward her and reached out for support from the back of an armchair that sat near the doorway. I stood there for a moment, hoping that wherever she took me wouldn't be a long journey.

I followed her into the next room, which led into another small, enclosed room. As I walked inside, I was impressed by the number of books lined up against the wall. They were all neat and uniform, tightly pressed so that they all fit perfectly in the bookcases. A large mahogany desk sat in the corner of the room. In the middle of the room were two chairs with a small table and a reading lamp nestled in between them.

"Sit down," she ordered me, pointing to one of the dark green armchairs, "and turn on that lamp so that I can see."

I obeyed her, turning on the lamp. The soft glow of the light made the room seem warm, but it felt rather stuffy. I found it almost difficult to breathe, but I was content to at least be able to sit.

The nun, after running her finger across a row of books, found what she was looking for and sat beside me in the adjacent armchair. She was silent, flipping through pages, obviously trying to find something she wished to show me.

I tried to make out the title of the book she held, but my reading wasn't very good at the time. I had learned the Polish alphabet, so I knew all the letters. But putting those letters together was often difficult. Plus, my head was throbbing, so I didn't try very hard before giving up.

"This is what I want to show you," she said through clenched teeth.

She held out the book in my direction. I turned toward her, only to find a grisly picture of a black beast with horns growing out of the sides of his skull. The beast was engulfed in flickering flames. His face was contorted, and he looked as though he were growling. I shuddered and looked away.

"This is hell," she stated rather calmly. "This is where you will be going because of what your father did to my people. To God's people! Do you see this black beast?" Her voice rose to a slightly higher pitch as she reached out and grabbed my chin, forcing me to look at the picture once more.

I stared at it, horrified.

"Do you see this black beast?" she screamed again, closing her hand tighter on my chin. I could feel her nails press into my skin.

Clearly she wanted an answer. I nodded. Of course I saw it. He was revolting.

Appeased by my response, she let go of my chin. I reached up and rubbed it, feeling the grooves where her nails had left marks.

"This is the black devil," she went on to explain. "One day this black devil will come for you. And when he does, he is going to take you straight into the fires of hell!"

I thought I would vomit right then. My body started shaking involuntarily.

"Take a good long look at this picture, boy, because soon you will call this place home. There is no hope for your soul. You are the product of the devil. You are the devil's son, and he will be coming to take you home!" she said as she thrust the book into my lap. It lay open, the devil staring straight at me.

I was so terrified by the gruesome picture and the fate the nun had bestowed upon me that I could barely breathe. I wanted to scream out loud: *But I don't know my father!*

I had no idea what he could have possibly done to this nun, but I knew that I didn't want to go to hell. I wasn't the one who had hurt her. I didn't even remember the war, let alone my father, so why should I have to pay for his sin? If she wanted my father to burn in hell with the black devil, that was fine with me. I didn't know the man. But there was no way that I wanted to be taken by the devil to a fiery end.

Tears gathered in the back of my throat, but I didn't want to let them loose. I didn't want to let the nun know how truly frightened I was. I wanted to run out of the room and away from the horrible orphanage, but I knew I was trapped. There was nowhere to go.

After all, this time the Soviets hadn't taken me away from Matka. Matka had brought me herself. Maybe she knew that this would be my lot in life. Maybe she knew I was the devil's child and believed that she had to give me away in order to save herself from a similar fate. Perhaps I did deserve to spend eternity in hell with the gruesome black beast with horns.

The nun and I sat in the library together for probably no more than an hour, but I felt like my entire life had been spent in that stuffy room. My body felt heavy, and my head was still throbbing. We sat in silence. She glared at me, so I was forced to sit and look at the horrifying picture on my lap.

Then we heard voices. They were light and cheery, penetrating the thick, suffocating silence in which the two of us sat. The nun sat up from her slumped state and grabbed the book out of my hands.

"Stand up! I will take you to your room with the rest of the children."

Without hesitating I arose from the reading chair, happy to have the chance to escape. I followed her out of the library and the adjacent room into a hallway, where the children's voices became more distinct. I inhaled a deep breath of fresh air. My legs were still shaking, but for now, at least, I was safe.

Chapter 8

Dieter arrived at the Catholic orphanage in Grudziądz a week later. I would like to say that life became more bearable once he arrived, but it grew worse. Though we never discussed it, I guessed that Dieter had been told something similar regarding his eternal fate in hell. He was prone to nightmares and crying out in the middle of the night. He often told me about the black beasts he saw in his dreams. They sounded like the same black beasts that visited me in the night.

Our nightmares were kind to us compared to the treatment we received. Both the nuns and the other children were intolerably cruel to Dieter. I thought I had heard all the insults possible at the previous orphanage, but the comments grew much worse at our supposed safe haven. Dieter's confidence seemed to diminish daily.

One afternoon we had been granted the unusual freedom to play outdoors rather than do chores. All of the children were excited and ran off into the yard and the surrounding woods to make use of their playtime. Dieter and I ran to the back part of the yard to play cowboys and Indians.

We pretended that we were both cowboys on the trail of a fierce Indian tribe. We found some sticks and carried them around like guns.

"I see one!" I yelled, cocking my gun in the direction of the woods. "Bang! Bang!"

"I don't think you got him," Dieter told me, aiming his stick in the same general direction.

"Bang! Bang!" he yelled, his gunshots a tad quieter than mine.

"You got him!" I screamed, jumping up and down.

"There's got to be more in the woods. Let's go find them!" he shouted excitedly.

I nodded in agreement as we made our way across the field toward the woods. I noticed some other boys out of the corner of my eye, but we were hot on the trail of Indians.

I ran ahead of Dieter and had almost entered the woods when I heard a loud *thwack* and the screams of Dieter behind me. I swirled around to find a couple of boys surrounding Dieter, who now lay on the ground.

"You ugly piece of no good Jew!" yelled the taller boy. He held a large stick, which he must have used to knock Dieter to the ground.

"Yeah! Who do you think you are to play on our field? You disgust me. Look at his eye and how it droops so low," commented the smaller boy. "Your mother must have been the ugliest woman alive." The two laughed.

My anger boiled. I was sick of everyone treating Dieter like an animal with no feelings.

"No, you two are ugly! Did you ever look in a mirror yourselves?" Dieter yelled back at them from the ground. He clutched his back where he had been hit, but he shed not a single tear.

"What did you say?" said the taller boy as he began to raise his stick. "Did you just talk back to us? What right do you, as a Jew, have to talk back to me? You are scum. You are nothing."

The smaller boy spit on Dieter.

Dieter had taken enough. His face turned red with anger; his eyes squinted into slits as he glared at the two boys hovering over him. He put one hand down on the ground to raise himself up to face his attackers, but as he did the taller boy came down hard on the top of Dieter's head with the stick. The smaller boy then jumped on him, swinging punches left and right.

Clutching the stick that had been serving as my cowboy gun, I charged at the two boys. I rammed myself into the taller one, knocking the stick out of his hand. I quickly picked his stick up, as it was much larger, and started swinging it at him. The smaller boy continued punching Dieter, who seemed to be unconscious from the blow to his head.

The taller boy punched and kicked at me, but I ignored him and lunged myself at the smaller boy. I knocked him off Dieter by punching him in the head. The smaller boy rolled off to the side and stood up, keeping his distance from me as I turned back toward the taller boy. I went in for another punch screaming, "Leave him alone! Why can't you just leave him alone?"

Some nuns ran outside in the meantime, grabbing both the taller boy and me before we could do any further damage.

"You devil child! Haven't you hurt us enough by being born into this world? Why must you cause more suffering?" the crazy nun I had encountered on my first day yelled as she dragged me into the building.

"They pick on Dieter! They were beating him with a stick!" I cried as she yanked me by the arm.

"He deserves a good beating, that ugly little Jewish beast. His people killed our Savior!"

She rushed me into the kitchen and had me stand in the corner while she went digging in the cupboard. She pulled out a bag of dried peas and spread them out onto the wood floor. They spilled every which way.

"Come and kneel down on these!"

I stood in the corner cowering, wiping my runny nose.

"Kneel down now before I have to force you!" she sneered at me through clenched teeth.

I obeyed, afraid of what other punishment she might try to inflict upon me.

The small, hard peas pierced my knees as I bent down and knelt on them. I could feel them indenting my skin, rubbing against my bone. To this day I have never felt such pain in my knees.

"Please, please, let me stand!" I pleaded.

"You will pay for your sins. You must be punished. Now kneel there until I say you may stand," she responded evenly.

A half an hour later, she had me stand. Dried peas stuck in both of my knees. Blood trickled down my legs as I picked them out of my skin one by one.

"Let this be a lesson to you," the nun hissed as she walked out of the room.

My skin showed the scabby, round circles for weeks afterward.

———————————————————

My stay at the Catholic orphanage grew even darker as the days progressed. I had thought that my first stay in the orphanage in Białochowo would be the most horrifying time in my life, but the nuns and priests taking care of us in Grudziądz were just as corrupt with lust.

A couple of months after my arrival, some of the nuns began to visit us during the night. Each one of them would select a child and bring him or her into another room. Once again, we were abused. Unlike the other orphanage, however, the same children were selected each time the nuns visited. The crazy nun always selected me.

She would come into the room after most of the children had fallen asleep, and she would rub my back. I always awoke with a start, knowing that tonight would be another night of crying myself to sleep.

I would get up and follow her out of the room and into the corridor, where we would either join other nuns and children in a room or be alone with one another in a secluded room at the other end of the building. Either way was torture. She molested me on more occasions than I care to remember.

On one particular night we were alone in one of the secluded rooms, and she ordered me to stand in the corner.

"Put your hands behind your back and your feet together," she snapped at me impatiently.

I did as she said mechanically. I knew the consequences could be severe if I didn't obey her orders. She came toward me, standing only in a thin robe, which fell open slightly to reveal one of her breasts.

"Raise your arms."

She slowly lifted the shirt I wore up over my head. I shivered, even though it was the middle of summer. Perhaps I shivered out of fear. She undid the buttons of my pants and slid them down, my underwear with them. Then she tied my hands together with a thin rope.

"Step out of the pants and stand still before me."

I obeyed, almost losing my balance since I didn't have my hands to help me remove them completely.

She stood back, examining me, and a sick smile formed on her face.

"Do you know why I selected you?" she sneered at me.

I didn't respond. I knew she would tell me regardless of my answer.

"Because you are the devil's spawn. You are pure evil and full of sin. There is nothing I could do to you that you wouldn't have chosen to do yourself." She laughed to herself as she drew closer to me.

She bent down before me and began touching and fondling me in places that I didn't like. I was so frightened and ashamed. I knew that what was happening to me was wrong, but there was little I could do. When she finished, she threw off her robe and revealed her naked body to me.

She walked over to the bed and lay flat on her back.

"Come now and please me," she hissed.

I slowly made my way toward her. As I approached, she sat up and grabbed my head, pulling my face close to hers.

"If you tell anyone about this...ANYONE...you will burn in hell for eternity!"

———————————————————

A few weeks later, the crazy nun came back for me in the middle of the night. This time she took me to a room with other nuns and children. Dieter was among them. As they each took their turn undressing us, they ridiculed us and called us filthy names. None of the children could bear to look around. We each felt shame in standing before the others.

The nuns proceeded to fondle us, and then several ordered us to fondle them. Only a few of the nuns were involved in these living nightmares, but a hatred toward them had begun to grow within me. The nun who selected me week after week was my main object of loathing.

During such moments when we were forced to do things that I knew were wrong, I used all the creativity of my 9-year-old mind to imagine scenarios of torture and suffering to inflict upon the crazy nun one day. I would make her suffer in the worst possible ways and then in one final scene, dispose of her completely. Not only had she harmed me physically, but she crippled me emotionally with her constant reminders of my future fate in hell. I didn't know whether to believe her or not. After all, she was completely crazy. But then again, she was a nun and knew all about heaven and hell. Either way, I couldn't care less whether I was going to hell or not. I just wanted to see her dead.

On this particular night, I considered drowning her. I could envision her gulping and gasping for air as I held her head just below the surface of the Wisła River. I had just about killed her when my scenario was shattered by the entrance of two priests.

I remember them distinctly. I overheard one of them speaking Russian, and the other one spoke Polish. For a moment I thought they might save us from the torture we were undergoing, but I was sorely mistaken. Instead, they sat quietly by, watching some of the nuns get fondled before they eventually joined in the molestation. The Soviet priest moved straight for Dieter, having him turn around so that his back was to him. The Polish priest moved toward me.

By the end of the night, the three to four children in the room had been molested by three nuns and raped by two priests.

— — — — — — — — — — — — — — — — —

I was not religious. My matka had taken me to church once, explaining to me everything I needed to know about God. She told me about His love for the world and how He sent His only Son to live among us, but that mankind killed Him with their stupidity and ignorance. She pointed at the large crucifix that hung over the altar. I stared at it, studying the sad man who hung from the two strips of wood that had been nailed together. I noted the blood, which poured out of his hands and his feet and dripped down his face from the crown of thorns stuck in his head.

"But why did we kill Him?" I asked.

"Because we were ignorant. But God knew that we would be, so He planned for the death of His Son ahead of time," she explained.

I sat still, puzzled why God would send His Son, knowing that He would suffer and eventually die. Matka must have seen the look of confusion on my face.

"Piotr, God's Son, Jesus, died so that we could go to heaven and be with Him forever. God forgave us. He forgave all of us who choose to believe."

I didn't understand then, but after a night of abuse from the nuns and priests, I reflected on what Matka had said. Maybe God would forgive me for my sins if I believed. But how could I believe? Wasn't it the nuns and priests who told my matka this? If so, then I was definitely going to hell, because the nuns told me that the fiery depths below would ultimately be my fate no matter what I did. I felt completely lost. Perhaps that was why Matka rarely took me to church, except for Christmas. She knew there would be no hope for me in heaven.

That night, in the depths of my sorrow, I decided I no longer wanted to live. If I was going to hell anyway, I might as well get things over with. Life was a living hell already. How much worse could it be with the devil?

I was still aching from the molestations. My body ached, but worse yet, I felt dead inside. I didn't know if Matka would ever come for me. It felt like I had been there forever. There didn't seem to be any way out. Every day meant more abuses. Besides, why would Matka come for me? I was the devil's child. No one would want to bring home an evil child. Not even my matka.

I was sitting in a room awaiting punishment for another fight when the nun I despised walked in. She stared intently at me, her eyes narrowing in on my face.

"You cannot help but do evil, can you?" she snarled at me from within the doorway.

Swift as a cat, she came toward me, lifting me up by both ears. She moved so quickly that I didn't know what was happening at first. Then, all of a sudden, I heard a loud ripping sound. I screamed, pain searing through my head. I felt the trickle of blood run down my neck. She had ripped my earlobe away from my head. I didn't think. I just reacted. I'm not sure what came over me, but I had taken enough.

I swirled around, arms flailing, slamming my fist into the nun's face. I could hear the bones in her nose crack as my knuckles made contact. She fell to the ground in a heap. I had completely knocked her out.

I stood over the woman. I thought to myself, *I could kill her.* After all, I had fantasized about it for months. Something stopped me, though. Perhaps it was the pain in my ear. Perhaps it was because other nuns ran into the room after hearing the commotion. But as I looked down at the woman below me, I felt nothing. There was no anger, no hatred, nothing. I was numb.

The other nuns dragged me out of the room, heaping insults on me as they carried me down the stairs. I didn't even try to put up a fight. They threw me in the cellar, where it was dark and musty. I didn't care. I was done with them. I was done with life.

I looked around the room. In the corner of the room was a small bed. Across from the bed sat a working bench. Above me was a wire hanging from a lamp in the ceiling. I sat on the bed and stared intently at the wire. The cord was thick and black. I lay there mesmerized as I recalled the cowboy movie that Dieter, Henryk and I had watched in Chełmno. I vividly remembered the swaying body of the dark cowboy. As I stood under the lamp, I realized that I had nothing to live for. I was like that cowboy, constantly being chased down. I didn't want to live like that anymore.

I got up from the bed, my head woozy from the pain in my ear, and managed to pick up the rickety bench and carry it over to the bed. I placed the bench on top of the bed and carefully climbed on top of it. I gingerly reached for the cord. Wrapping it around my neck, I looked around the room one last time.

"Goodbye, Mamusiu."

I kicked the bench out from under me, letting it crash to the ground. For one brief moment I hung suspended above the ground, legs dangling, gasping for air. The next thing I knew I was on the ground, my body in spasms as the lamp was pulled from the ceiling by my weight. I suffered an intense electric shock, my arms and legs shaking as the electric current ran through my body. The dim light of the lamp went out, and I was in complete darkness. I had blown a fuse.

As I lay there in shock, I was aware that there was someone else in the room. The cellar was no longer dark, but illuminated by a bright light. A face appeared before me and for the first time since I had arrived at the orphanage, I experienced an encompassing sense of tranquility. God had sent an angel to bring me the peace I needed to stay alive. Perhaps there was a reason for living after all.

Not long after my suicide attempt, my Uncle Franek arrived with two other soldiers. The three of them had a commanding presence. They demanded that I be allowed to leave with them. After showing the nuns some documents, they picked me up and rescued me from the orphanage. I couldn't walk by myself, so Franek took me directly to the hospital. There I had another operation to repair the damage from the abuses I had endured.

Though I was thrilled to leave the orphanage, it was a bittersweet goodbye. Dieter had to stay another couple of months without me before his caretaker was able to provide the documents needed to release him. I thought about him every day, hoping that no one would bully him. I hoped he would be able to come home to Toruń soon.

I was home with my matka, though. And she happily informed me that the Catholic orphanage was the last orphanage I would ever have to go to. I didn't understand then, but I later learned that my matka had obtained the necessary paperwork to adopt me. I was no longer an orphan. I was Piotr Szczepański Loth, and that meant I was safe from harm.

A picture of my birth mother before she was
arrested by the Danzig Gestapo

S.S. headquarters and the main gate to
Stutthof Concentration Camp

Children's prison in Toruń where I was held
before being taken to the orphanages

Revisiting the Toruń train station

Białochowo orphanage – main building

Białochowo orphanage – smaller building where Star and I stayed

Lake behind the smaller orphanage where Star and I would play

Picture of orphans at the Białochowo orphanages. I am the boy in the first row, all the way to the left. Star is on the other side of the girl next to me. Although I don't actually remember wearing a star on my own shirt, you can see it in this picture that my matka gave me. Even after the war, it seems that the Jewish children were labeled in this way. I can think of no other explanation for our having to wear these stars.

Me and Matka

Tower in the fortress wall where Matka and I lived

Open area where the gypsies camped

Picture of my sisters, Barbara and Georgia,
that I received in the mail

Prison where I was held, interrogated, and beaten
by the KGB for being a "spy"

Fortress wall from which Henryk and I watched operations taking place in the hospital to the left

TRAVEL PERMIT OFFICE FOR GERMANY

WARSZAWA, JEZUICKA 2

2.1.59

Betrifft: Reise in die Bundesrepublik Deutschland.

P. Peter Oswald CZECHOPANSKA (LOTH)
Torun
Fosa Staromiejska 26

1) Das „Travel Permit Office" ist ermächtigt worden, Ihnen eine Einreise in die Bundesrepublik Deutschland zu genehmigen.

2) Bei Vorlage eines gültigen Reisepasses oder eines anderen anerkannten Reiseausweises wird der erforderliche Sichtvermerk (Visum) erteilt.

1) Biuro nasze zostało upoważnione do wydania przepustki do Niemieckiej Republiki Federalnej.

2) Po przedstawieniu ważnego (ych) paszportu (ów) lub innego (ych) ważnego (ych) dokumentu (ów) podróży zostanie (q) wydana (e) wiza (y).

UWAGA:
Przy zgłoszeniu się z paszportem do wizowania, należy podać numer listy—Listen—Nummer Po/ 6087 wjazd na stałe
Biuro czynne codziennie, z wyjątkiem sobót i świąt od godz. 9.00 do 12.30 i 13.30—15.30.

Travel permit allowing me to enter Germany in 1959. At the bottom, in Polish, it is written that I can "never return."

Me, Val, Phillip, Sandy, and Juliana in Europe – 2002

Chapter 9

Life settled down after my last stay at the orphanage. Matka and I moved to a new place in the middle of town. Before the war the apartment had served as a storefront, but the business quickly went under when the Soviets brought Communism into Poland. Since the end of the war, people had moved in and out of the space, transforming it into a livable home. And now it was ours.

The place was a little bigger than our last one and had a large, open room, a backroom, and a basement below. And though I was a little sad to leave our home in the tower, the move meant extra income for us. Matka was able to divide up our one large room and rent the tiny spaces out to people. Our home was always full — at any given time there were four or five other people living with us. Matka liked it that way.

Our new home was in a great location, just around the corner from various shops. It was also closer to the old military bunkers that surrounded our town. The bunkers jutted up from the landscape, leaving large mounds of dirt and grass that soldiers hid behind during battles. Though the war had been over for several years, digging deep enough could yield tons of treasures that any boy would love to get his hands on.

I would meet Henryk, Dieter, and a couple of other friends at the bunker nearly every day to try and dig up artifacts from the war. We had found several pistols, grenades, boots, and uniforms — sometimes with skeletons still in them. We usually divvied up the spoils, each boy taking a part of the loot home with him to play with and hold for safekeeping.

"Henryk! Help me dig over here. I think I found something big!" I yelled at the top of my lungs one day after several hours of searching. I was diligently trying to dig out a large, black object that refused to budge.

Henryk scurried over to where I was crouched.

"What is it?" he asked.

"I don't know, but I think it's big. Go on that side and help me dig it out."

I had managed to unearth a portion of the object, but the other side was still completely buried in hard-packed dirt. Henryk started digging furiously. He uncovered most of the other side in half the time it had taken me to do the same.

"I think it's an old bomb!" Henryk cried out excitedly.

The two of us stood over it, looking down at the dirt-encrusted sphere. It was a bomb. It had to be.

"We've got to get this home! Wouldn't it be great to set it off?" I said.

Our other friends scrambled up to where we stood.

"How are you going to get it home?" one of them asked.

I didn't have an answer at first. I just knew that this had to come home with me. If we left it at the bunkers, then someone might find it and take it. I didn't spend two hours of my life digging to let someone else take my treasure. Besides, it wasn't just any treasure. This was the treasure of all treasures.

"What if we use my wagon?" I said, suddenly remembering the little red wagon Matka and I used to carry our groceries home.

"Yeah! That will do it. Come on, let's go get it," Henryk yelled excitedly.

"Okay, you two stay here with the bomb while Henryk and I go get the wagon."

The other boys nodded as Henryk and I ran down the cobbled streets to my home. We laughed and talked excitedly the whole way there. This was by far the best thing we had ever found.

When Henryk and I returned, the four of us heaved the bomb into the wagon as best as we could. It was pretty heavy, even for the four of us. The bomb clanged against the sides of the wagon, but it was in there. We had our treasure.

In no time, the four of us were back at my house, where we dragged the bomb down into my basement. Matka was chatting away with one of our gossipy renters, only murmuring to us to be careful not to hurt ourselves as we played down there. She had no idea how many grenades, pistols, and bullets I had in the basement already. Now we were adding a bomb to the collection.

"Drag it over to this corner over here," one of the boys directed us.

We did as he said, pushing and pulling the heavy object out of direct eyesight. No one would notice it in the corner. If they did, they probably wouldn't think it was a bomb. After all, who keeps bombs in their basement?

"Let's see if we can pry it open. I always wondered what kind of powder is in a bomb," the other boy said.

He wasn't the only one; we all wanted to know what was inside the bomb.

"Here's a crowbar. This might do," Henryk said, handing the tool to one of the boys. We all searched the basement for something that might work to pry open the bomb. Then each of us took turns beating the bomb with our crowbars. Some of us pushed, others pulled, but nothing happened. The bomb wouldn't budge.

"Maybe if I get on top of it and pull," I said, trying to think of another way to get inside.

I climbed up on top with my crowbar in hand. I slammed down hard on the bomb several times. The constant hammering and pounding was beginning to give me a headache, but I really wanted to get inside that bomb.

"Piotr! What are you boys doing down there?" Matka called from above.

We froze in our tracks.

"Just playing war, Matka," I yelled back up to her.

"Well, stop it already. You are giving Agnieska a headache. Come up here and have some dinner. You boys can play tomorrow."

The four of us looked at each other.

"We'll try again tomorrow," I whispered.

We promised not to tell a soul about our new find. We didn't want to risk others finding out and taking it away from us. We were going to discover what was inside the bomb if it was the last thing we did.

———————————————

The very next day the authorities knocked on our door, demanding to see what was in our basement.

"Certainly. May I ask why?" Matka said, unsure why the Polish police wished to see her basement.

"It seems that your son, madam, has been hiding some weapons down there," the policeman said sternly, glancing in my direction. "Now if you don't mind, we're going to see for ourselves."

The policemen made their way down to the basement and began searching. They pulled out my pistols and grenades from their hiding places before finally stumbling across our bomb in the corner.

I never saw such fear cross the faces of two seemingly overconfident men. One cursed as the other backed away.

"How did you get a bomb down here?" the one yelled at me, grabbing a hold of the back of my shirt.

"The wagon," I said, suddenly realizing how much trouble I was in.

"Do you know what this bomb could do if it went off?" he yelled, not waiting for a response. The intensity of his voice began to frighten me.

"This bomb could take out the whole block if it detonated! You would have killed hundreds of innocent people with your childish games."

He pulled me in front of him and hit me in the mouth.

"You idiot child!"

He threw me at my matka, who gave me a look that could kill.

I cowered in fear. These men were scared; and now all of a sudden, so was I.

"We've got to get this out of here, and we've got to do so carefully. And I suggest that you, madam, teach this boy a lesson."

The two policemen began making a plan as more men streamed down into the basement to help remove the bomb.

Matka and I were ordered out of the house. The whole block was evacuated until they were able to remove the bomb safely, which they did after several long hours.

In the meantime, Matka taught me her lesson. She beat me with an umbrella until I was black and blue. Then she held me tightly, crying.

"Piotr, Piotr. You silly boy! You could have killed us all. You survived for this? No, you must be smart, Piotr. You must live!"

If I ever deserved to be beaten, that was it. And I knew it. I never did find out how the authorities knew about our stash. But I do know that I wasn't the only boy beaten by his mother that night.

———————————————————

Though the authorities took most of the treasures we had collected, my friends and I were able to find more trouble to get into. Our collection gradually began to rebuild itself, but as our interests began to vary, we spent time spying on people and things we probably should not have been watching. We were at the brink of adolescence, with most of us about 12 years old, so we were free to roam the streets of Toruń as we liked.

Henryk and I were out exploring by the fortress wall one day when we heard screaming like we had never heard before. We looked all around us trying to figure out where the woman's screams were coming from, but we were stumped.

"Do you think someone is beating her?" Henryk asked.

"I don't know," I said, "but we should find out where she is."

The screams stopped. Three minutes later, they began again.

"I think it's in that building way down there! Doesn't it sound like the screams are coming from there?" Henryk asked as he ran toward the noise.

"That's the hospital."

We approached the old, red brick building and craned our necks to see if we could look in any of the windows.

"She's got to be in one of those rooms on the top. It sounds like the screams are coming from up high," he said, pointing to the top of the four-story building.

"Want to see what's wrong with her?" I asked Henryk excitedly.

"Yeah?"

"Well, I've got an idea. Follow me!"

I headed in the direction of the fortress walls, which were directly across from the hospital.

"Let's climb!" I said smiling, remembering our conversation about climbing up these walls back when we were in the orphanage. We were finally going to do it together.

The two of us climbed to the top of the wall in no time. The view was spectacular. On one side you could see the Wisła River, and on the other side you could see almost the entire town. More importantly, however, the walls were just high enough for us to see directly into the operating room of the hospital.

In the room we could see doctors rushing around a poor woman as she clenched a pillow tight to her chest and screamed.

"What's happening?" Henryk asked, in awe of the scene before him.

"I don't know, but she's in pain!"

We sat there for the next two hours before we realized what was happening. The woman eventually gave birth to what looked like a baby boy. Henryk and I were repulsed and amazed all at the same time. Either way, we were addicted.

We spent countless hours sitting on that fortress wall, watching all sorts of amazing things happen within that tiny operating room. There was little to no electricity in our town at that time, so all operations had to be done in the daylight. Since the doctors needed the light to operate, they never bothered to close any of the windows. From our perch on the wall, Henryk and I saw births, operations, and even deaths. We learned all about life from our time on that wall.

— — — — — — — — — — — — — — — —

Matka and I moved to yet another home, which was located right across the street from the theater. This new apartment was our best one yet. Not only did we have our own room and living space, but we also had a kitchen with a working gas stove. Matka loved cooking over her new stove. Plus, it was rumored that the building was located right next door to where the famous astronomer Nicolaus Copernicus had once lived and carried out his studies. Rumor also had it that the building I lived in was actually the house where Copernicus was born. The house had since been divided up into apartments, so everyone who lived in our building reveled in this claim to fame.

And while the history behind the house where I lived was intriguing to say the least, the whole neighborhood was wonderful. I lived right around the corner from my friend, Henryk, and his family. My next-door neighbor was a young girl named Renata, who would often join my friends and me on various adventures. But the best part about my new home was its close proximity to the Opera House. The theater had shows during the evening, so we could regularly hear the beautiful music from our apartment. I often fell asleep listening to the voices stream in through my window.

Henryk and I used to prowl the grounds of the Opera House, looking for ways to get inside without paying. One time we managed to slide in the back door without being noticed. We could hear the music from onstage, but we quickly realized we were backstage with all of the performers. We tried to find our way through the maze of curtains and props in the darkness and ended up near the ladies' dressing rooms. We caught a glimpse before being discovered and thrown out on our behinds.

Dieter, Henryk, and I always managed to find trouble, particularly as our interests turned to the opposite sex. The girls liked Henryk and me all right, but poor Dieter could never get a date. In fact, most girls couldn't even bear to look at his face. Renata was the only girl who would talk to him. I always felt awful about that, but there was nothing I could do.

One time we were hanging out in the town square when another group of kids approached us. For a while we all talked and mingled, but then one of the new girls started making fun of Dieter. The other kids laughed, so she became even crueler with her words. I could see Dieter begin to shake with each new insult. I stood up and told the girl to be quiet, but she ignored me. Finally, Dieter couldn't take it any longer, and he burst into tears, which only fueled the fire of insults being thrown at him. Without a word, he got up and ran away, crying the entire time.

I was furious. I had never been so angry in my entire life, mostly because I knew how embarrassed Dieter must have felt to cry in front of the girl. Normally I would have fought the person insulting Dieter, but I knew I couldn't punch a girl. Still, I wanted revenge. No one would say such hateful things if they knew Dieter. He was the kindest soul you could ever meet. He would never do anyone harm. That is why I had to concoct a plan.

The next day, Dieter and I made our way over to the girl's home at dusk. The neighborhood was quiet. Families were probably just sitting down for dinner. We looked to see if there was anyone in sight before we made our move. Feeling certain that no one was around, we quickly pulled down our pants and each took a satisfying poop on the doorstep. We had trouble keeping our laughter to ourselves, but we managed to complete the task without being caught. We then knocked on the door and ran quickly across the street. The girl's father walked out of the house.

"Did you boys knock on our door?" he yelled across the street, not noticing that he was standing in our poop.

We never answered his question. Instead, we threw insults at him and his daughter. He cursed at us, telling us we were trouble-makers up to no good. Then he turned around and walked right back into his house, our poop stuck to his shoes. Who knows how long it took to get the stench out of their carpets.

After all the torment in our short lives, revenge felt good. And that wasn't our only act of retribution. Dieter and I were hanging out with our friends another time when a couple of guys joined us. One of them started making fun of Dieter for the way he looked. Dieter gave him a smart reply, which made the guy so angry that he swung at Dieter, hitting him squarely in the side of the head. I wasn't quick enough to stop the blow, but I lunged toward the guy and tried to hit him. He saw me coming and punched me in the face, sending me to the ground. He and his friends spit at us and then walked away, thinking they had achieved something.

What they didn't realize was that at nearly 12 years old, I was a master at revenge. No one got the last word against my friends or me. I told Dieter and Henryk to steal a couple of eggs from their pantries and hide them someplace so that they would rot. I took a few from Matka and did the same. That Sunday we met up and gathered all of the rotten eggs we had collected during the week. We got up relatively early, so we could be at the kid's house before they had all woken up. Once there, we quietly climbed up on his roof. We sat there for what seemed like hours before the kid and his family came out their door. They were all dressed up like they were going somewhere nice. My friends and I looked at each other and smiled. This was too good to be true.

Without so much as a warning, we began hurling the rotten eggs, along with some choice insults, at the unsuspecting family below us. The women screamed, and the men cursed at us. They were so confused and disgusted by the stench of the rotten eggs that they quickly ran back inside their house. Somehow we were able to get away with our plan without being pummeled.

Maybe there were better ways to handle the cruelty of those around us, but life hadn't shown us the high road. Instead, life had taught us about suffering, irrational hatred, and the danger of being utterly alone in a hostile world. To survive, we had to band together.

I was never afraid to stick up for Dieter. He was my best friend, so I would do anything for him. He managed to hold his own most of the time. But when his spirit was broken from all the insults and hateful things people said to him about his appearance, I had to step up and defend him. He was an orphan; he didn't have parents to defend him. His mother and father had died in the war, so someone had to be there for him.

I felt this way toward all of my close friends. I would do anything for them. They were my family. Dieter and Henryk were the brothers I never had. In a way, I felt as though we were even closer than brothers, because we chose each other. And I knew that either one of them would have done anything for me. We were true friends, and nothing would ever change that.

Chapter 10

As the fear of having to go back to another orphanage faded into a memory and I settled into a halfway normal life, my dreams and aspirations for the future began to take shape. As much as I loved my matka and friends, I knew there were greater adventures in store for me. My beloved Toruń would always be home to me, but I couldn't imagine staying forever. When I watched the adults in my town and saw the various destinies awaiting the average Polish boy, I knew I wasn't like them — I was going to be a gypsy king.

The hope of one day traveling the world with the gypsies kept me going. As I interacted with my neighbors and friends or when someone picked a fight with me, the fact that I would one day be a gypsy king was tucked safely in the back of my mind. Such hope made me feel free.

Of course, the reality was that the Polish people were anything but free. We were under strict Soviet control. Our conversations, newspapers, correspondence — all were monitored by the Soviets. Poland was in such an oppressive state that every letter sent by regular post was opened and read by the government. Anything the government didn't like was censored — blotted or even cut out of the letter.

So instead of corresponding through the mail, Matka sent all of her letters through the gypsies. Our contact with the gypsies was the one way around Soviet control. The gypsies would deliver her letters in exchange for something, which differed every time, and it was pretty much guaranteed that the letter would arrive safely at its destination.

One day, however, I received a package in the regular post. I had never received a package before, so I was quite excited to see what was inside. The letter with it was written in German, so Matka read the letter and told me the package was from the Red Cross. I didn't really know what that meant nor did I care; I was more interested in the contents. There was powdered milk, powdered eggs, women's nylons, and some flour. I could tell that half of the package was missing, the items rummaged through before it had ever reached our doorstep, but I was thrilled.

After methodically looking over every item, Matka decided to keep some of the powdered milk and powdered eggs. She had no trouble exchanging the rest of the items for various goods we could use around the house. The nylons, in particular, could be traded for all sorts of food and vegetables. Nylons were a hot commodity in Poland, because very few stores stocked them. Matka and I felt like royalty.

Shortly after receiving the package, my fourteenth birthday arrived. My previous birthdays had come and gone without much excitement, but this day was special. On this day — September 2, 1957 — I would be free to do what I pleased, go where I pleased, and live how I pleased. It was the day I was to become the gypsy king's son.

I spent all day dreaming about the night's events. I thought about the dancing and the food and the final goodbyes to my friends. I would no longer be a simple Polish boy. Instead I was to become a world traveler. I could only dream of the stories I might have to share after a year's worth of traveling about with the gypsies.

Matka was gone most of the day, so I spent some time playing with Dieter. I didn't know where she was; I assumed she was preparing for my special day. I figured she would want to make everything perfect for my birthday celebration. In the meantime, Dieter and I dreamt up new adventures for me, and I promised to bring back treasures from each of my destinations.

That evening, Matka finally returned from her long outing. I had just finished gathering a few things to bring with me to the camp, because I wasn't sure when the gypsies were planning to pack up and go on their next journey. I wanted to be prepared to leave with them. When I looked up at her from where I sat amidst my pile of belongings, I could tell from her tear-streaked cheeks that Matka had been crying.

"What's wrong?" I asked, concerned that something bad had happened to her while doing her errands.

She didn't respond. Instead, she turned her head and started sobbing. I had never seen her so upset before. I figured it must have something to do with the fact that I would be leaving her to join the gypsies. Her crying bothered me, though, because I thought she would be happy for me. Why couldn't she just be happy that I would be going off on spectacular adventures to see the world?

Feeling a bit annoyed, I ignored her cries and told her that I was ready to go to the camp. Matka rubbed her nose with a handkerchief and gathered a few things before heading out the door. We made our way down the steps and out into the fresh air. I hadn't realized how stuffy it was in the house. I couldn't wait to be a gypsy and always have the opportunity to be in the fresh air.

As we stepped out onto the cobbled streets, I surveyed my neighborhood and realized that it would no longer be my home. I was surprised at the pang of sadness that struck me. Since I wasn't sure if it would be my last night in Toruń, I thought it would be nice to cut through town and walk along the Wisła River. Matka consented, and we made our way along the river.

I'll never forget how beautiful that night was as we walked. The sun was just setting beneath the trees along the side of the river. Rays of orange and yellow poked through the leaves of the trees, bouncing brilliant colors off the slowly moving Wisła. There was no one else about, only Matka and me walking quietly to the best night of my life, or so I thought.

We soon found ourselves entering the gypsy camp. The sun was just dipping below the last trees, allowing the darkness of the night to slowly encroach upon us. People were milling about, cooking, eating and laughing near the brightly burning fire. Several men and women were dancing rhythmically to the fast music being played.

They all came to celebrate my birthday. As I surveyed the scene, I felt a strong sense of pride. These people were now my family.

I stood near the fire for a moment, breathing in the delicious aroma of cooking meat and feeling the warmth of the fire against my skin. Being in the camp just felt right. Standing by the fire, mesmerized by the flickering flames, I saw the gypsy king approaching. I could sense Matka tense up beside me, but I immediately stepped back from the fire and ran toward the king. He smiled at me, grabbing me by the shoulders and pulling me in for a kiss. I felt an enormous love for him. He was saving me from the world around me. He was going to grant me a life outside of the pain I had always known.

The gypsy king looked past me and spotted Matka. The two shared a knowing look, which annoyed me. Their glances had always meant the same thing: they were keeping something from me.

"Come, let's go inside for a moment. Your matka has something she needs to tell you," the gypsy king said as he motioned for me to follow them into the tent.

I began to get an uneasy feeling in the pit of my stomach, but I obediently followed behind him. We sat inside the tent, the gypsy king on one side of me and my matka on the other.

Grabbing my hand, Matka took a deep breath before beginning. Tears started streaming down her face before she even spoke.

"Piotrusiu, there is something I have kept from you all of these years. I am not your real mother. I have been taking care of you so that one day you would be able to meet your real mother. I did my best to try to protect you from harm, because I loved you. You may not be my son by birth, but you are and always will be my son. But you have a real mother who lives in Germany."

I pulled my hand away, repulsed by the words I heard, unwilling to believe them.

"Piotr, your mother wants to meet you. She's been waiting a long time for you. She finally responded to my letters. You need to go to Germany, where you will really be free. You can't stay with the gypsies."

My heart beat so fast I could feel it pounding against my chest. My world started caving in. My matka didn't love me anymore. Why else would she be saying this to me?

"Matka, what are you talking about?" I cried. "Is it that you don't love me anymore? You don't want me anymore, Mamusiu?" Tears now streamed down my face.

"No, Piotrusiu. I will always love you until the day I die. I will always be your matka, but you have a real mother who loves you too." She paused for a moment, trying to collect herself before continuing. "The reason I didn't tell you was because I was trying to protect you."

Matka sat there in silence, waiting for my response. The only thing I heard, though, was that my matka no longer loved me. She had lied to me my entire life. I didn't know who I was or where I was from.

My world was over. I didn't care about the gypsy party. I didn't care about anything.

"I'm sorry, Piotr. But I received a letter today, and it says that you need to go to Germany. That's why I'm telling you this now. I'm so sorry," she cried, reaching out for me.

I pulled away quickly.

"I don't know what you are talking about, and I don't care!" I yelled, snot running down my nose and onto my shirt.

I ran out of the tent. I ran past the bright fire and dancing gypsies. I ran along the dark path beside the Wisła River. I ran across the bridge that led to the old, abandoned castle along the river. I found my way inside the castle, inching my way along the dark tunnels leading to the basement below.

There I sat, finally. I was out of breath and all alone. I wept. I didn't understand what Matka was trying to tell me. How could she not be my mother? Who was my real mother then? And why had she abandoned me? Why didn't anyone love me?

———————————————————

I hid out in the castle for almost a week. Henryk, Dieter, and some of my other friends knew where I was hiding, so they would visit me and bring me food. They kept me updated on what was happening back in town.

On the third day of hiding, Henryk informed me that the gypsies had packed up their camp and headed out of town already. I felt sick to my stomach. I was supposed to be with them. My chance at freedom was gone. My dreams were shattered. All I wanted to do was curl up and die.

A few days later, Henryk came back to tell me that he had run into my matka. I missed my matka, even though I wouldn't admit it to my friends. Henryk obviously felt sorry for her and told me that she had been crying. He tried to persuade me that Matka really did love me, but I wasn't too sure. People had let me down my whole life. I just never thought Matka would be one of them.

Henryk did a decent job convincing me to go home. Even though I was angry, I missed Matka. I didn't like being alone out there in that big, empty, bombed-out castle across the river. So I gave in and made my way back home.

I walked in the door without so much as a word. Matka was cooking over the stove. I could tell she had been crying. When she realized I was standing in the doorway, she dropped her spoon and ran toward me, pulling me into her.

"Piotr, my Piotrusiu! I love you! I love you," she sobbed.

I cried too. As much as I was angry and wanted to resist letting her know I had missed her, I could not.

Matka pulled me away from her, holding my shoulders firmly and looking directly into my eyes so that I couldn't look away.

"You have to go so you can be free," she told me.

"But, Matka," I argued, "I don't know this woman. How can I go to this person I don't know? If she really wants me, then why would she have left me behind?"

Matka slowly let go of my shoulders and wiped one of the tears from my cheek.

"She had to," she replied.

And that's all she said. That was her answer. My real mother had to leave me. That explanation made no sense to me. I couldn't understand why anyone would have to leave her child behind.

At that moment, I began to hate the woman who had abandoned me. I hated her for leaving me to suffer in the orphanages all those years. Most of all, I hated her for disrupting my life just when it was starting to be livable. I learned to curse her name. I became very bitter toward her, so much so that the thought of her would send me into a silent rage. I would never understand how a woman could abandon her child the way she had.

And while I was with my Polish matka, living in her home until I was to be sent to Germany, I was angry with her, too. She was making me go to Germany to meet some woman I didn't know and couldn't care less about. And while she said she loved me, I had to wonder how she could stand to send me away. My life had always been tumultuous, but I had always had my matka to rely upon. Now I didn't know if I could even trust her.

———————————————

After a few months, life sort of moved on. We had to wait for our paperwork to clear before being allowed to make the trip to Germany, so I pretended that the journey would never happen. While we waited, Matka was able to make some money as a cleaning woman, so I would tag along and help her out from time to time.

My favorite place to clean was the bakery. The one we went to most often sold Russian baked goods. While Matka cleaned, I would go through the trash and pick out the icing decorators. Then, after our long day of cleaning, we would bring all the goodies home. I'd sit on the front steps with my friends, passing the different flavors of icing back and forth between us. And even though there was sawdust and bits of trash stuck to the decorators, every one of us had icing smeared across our faces. It was just too good to resist.

On one of the days we spent cleaning, I received a letter through the regular post. The letter had been censored, so a lot of it was either missing or blotted out. Inside the letter I found a picture of two little girls. They were very pretty, but there was something different about the way they looked. They were darker than anyone I had ever seen before, even darker than Henryk. Matka read the back of the picture, which said "Georgia" and "Barbara" and then had "mother" and "love", but the other words were crossed out. Even though I couldn't read the writing on the back, I took the picture and kept it with me. Since the letter had been tampered with, neither Matka nor I knew exactly who those girls were, but I knew they were special.

From time to time the gypsies would come with more letters from my birth mother and the Red Cross, but the last letter we received by regular post came from the U.S. Army base in Baumholder, Germany — yet another censored message written in a language I didn't understand.

Two days later, Matka and I heard a loud knock on our door just after dinner. We knew the drill and quickly realized that the individuals behind the door weren't friendly visitors. However, we had no choice but open the door. Matka had paperwork that would keep me from being sent to another orphanage, so she felt confident that no one could take me away.

She was wrong.

As she opened the door, several Polish police officers rushed in and swiftly placed handcuffs on me. Without any explanation they dragged me out of our apartment. I remember asking why I was being arrested, but they told me to shut up if I knew what was good for me. I did as they said.

The officers took me to the police station, where they began hounding me with questions. I sat at a table in a small room, while one officer after another harassed me with questions.

"Who do you know at the American base?" they asked.

"I don't know."

"You received a letter from the base, did you not?"

"Yes."

"Well, who do you know there, then?" they shouted.

"I don't know!" I said. I remembered Matka receiving the letter and reading it to herself, but she was so secretive. She never explained why the letter arrived from an American base. I just accepted the fact without thinking much about it. I wished I had asked more questions then.

"What are you hiding from us, boy?" they shouted in my ear.

"Nothing, sir!"

"You are a liar!" They threw me to the floor. "Listen, boy, you better tell us the truth now, because we're the nice ones. If you don't tell us the truth, the KGB officers will come…"

I wished that I could tell them something, but I really didn't know a thing about the letter from the American base. Had I known what was to come, I might have lied to them.

The KGB arrived and took me to another prison where they interrogated me for hours on end, asking me the same questions over and over again. My answers never changed, because I still didn't know the information they were so desperately seeking. Finally, they had listened to enough of what they perceived as my lies. They sat me down in a chair and began beating me until my face and body felt numb.

"What do you know about these Americans?" one officer screamed at me. "Are you a spy for the United States? Did you think you could get away with trying to spy on us?"

I was unable to answer, exhausted from the hours of questioning.

"Answer me, boy!" the officer said as he smashed his fist into my jaw. I tasted the blood in my mouth, my eyes a mess of wet tears.

"I'm just a kid," I said. "How could I know anything about these Americans? I never met an American in my life."

My pleas went unnoticed.

"You are a traitor and a liar!"

With that, one officer took the butt of his rife and slammed it into my stomach. I fell backwards out of the chair, collapsing on the floor. I struggled for air, thinking that the next blow might be the end of me. The KGB agents picked me up off the ground and set me against the wall, a better position for their renewed assaults on my head and the side of my face. Blood streamed out of my mouth, and I could feel my back teeth wiggle out of place. I nearly gagged on one of my molars. Soon after, I passed out.

The next few days I endured more of the same, until they finally put me in a room by myself. I stayed there for several weeks, locked up without seeing the light of day. I didn't understand why they were so insistent. I really didn't know anyone from the United States.

And then one day, out of the blue, they told me I would be released soon. They gave me a long bath and took me to a doctor who cared for the wounds from their constant beatings. I was completely confused. Just a few weeks ago they had been beating me. Now all of a sudden they were taking care of me, trying to conceal my injuries.

One evening an officer explained why they had decided to finally release me.

"We've been informed that you are a German child, and your birth mother wants you with her. Therefore, you are being sent back to Germany soon. You'll need to get your paperwork in order before you leave."

And without so much as a goodbye or an apology for having beaten me unconscious, the police officers released me into the care of my matka.

Chapter 11

W hen I came home from the interrogations, Matka had sold everything. She explained that we needed all the money we could get if we were going to travel to Germany.

"Matka, why can't I just stay here with you? I don't need to go to Germany," I said. I was sick of hearing about Germany. I didn't want to go to Germany. I didn't want to go anywhere. I just wanted to stay where I felt comfortable. I didn't understand why everyone was making such a big deal about going to Germany.

"Piotr, it is too late. You have no choice anymore. You have to go to Germany. They won't let you stay here, even if you beg and plead. It is for the best, I promise. God knows what is best."

I didn't argue with her. I knew I didn't have a choice. I didn't think she was right in saying it would be better for me, but I knew no amount of arguing would change her mind.

Within a month or so, Matka and I made our first trip to Warsaw, Poland. The trip by train was long and arduous. We didn't have the money we needed to take a taxi around the large city when we arrived, so we had to walk to and from the German and Polish embassies.

Both places were confusing. We never seemed to have the right paperwork in order. One place would tell us one thing, and the other would tell us something completely different. I could sense Matka becoming agitated, but she explained that it would be no use getting angry with government officials. She told me that it was just part of the process to make people run around town. Government officials got a kick out of making poor people flustered. She was right. By the end of the day, they told us we had to go back home to get things straightened out and come back at another time. So we called it a day and took our third-class train ticket back home.

Over the next few months, we went back to Warsaw a second and third time. Our money was swiftly running out, and we could barely afford the trips there and back. There was some mix-up with government officials needing to change my name from Piotr Szczepański Loth to Peter Loth. The Germans had such a difficult time spelling "Szczepański" that we had to go back a couple of times just to get that right.

After our last trip to Warsaw, we realized that we didn't have enough money to get back to Toruń, so we hitchhiked. I remember climbing in the back of a wagon and riding along for two hours before we were dropped off. Then we walked for several kilometers before a truck stopped to pick us up. We hitchhiked and walked all the way back to Toruń, a distance of 150 kilometers.

On the bright side, it was fun spending time with Matka. But it made me hate having to leave for Germany even more. As we walked and rode, she told me how much better my life could be outside of Poland. She told me of the beautiful countryside of Germany and the opportunities that I would have by living there. I tried to believe her, but my heart belonged to Poland.

After we returned from our last trip to Warsaw, I noticed that my friends began to act differently around me. We used to have so much fun and adventure, but they had grown sad and depressed as my departure became a reality. Plus, I found a girlfriend in between my trips to Warsaw, and she cried every time Germany was mentioned. It seemed like our worlds were ending.

I knew then that I would be leaving for sure. Dealing with all the paperwork made it real for me. So I decided that I would get Dieter to promise to take care of my girlfriend, Ursula. At first she was very hesitant. After all, she was a beautiful girl. And Dieter, of course, was different from the rest of us. Ursula was very kind, though. Eventually she relented, and the two spent more time together. They went on dates and began to enjoy each other's company. I promised them that when I arrived in Germany, I would send them all sorts of gifts, whatever they wished. In return, they told me they would name their children after me. They were young and in love, which made me happy. I wanted Dieter to be happy when I left. I couldn't bear the thought of him being left alone in this world. He needed someone he could take care of and who would take care of him.

During the time of transition with my friends, I received a permit by mail that stated that I was to leave Poland immediately. Not only was I to leave, but I was to leave forever. The permit stated that I would never be able to return to Poland again. I didn't quite understand what that meant, but my main concern was whether I would have to go to Germany alone.

When I asked Matka if she was coming to Germany with me, she said yes. With that assurance, I grew excited at the prospect of traveling to a new place. I had always wanted to travel. Perhaps this would be my first real adventure. And Matka would be there with me every step of the way, which made it all the better — a benefit that not even the gypsies had offered.

If I had known the truth, I probably would have run away for good. Matka never really told me the truth. She loved me too much and knew that if she explained everything to me, I would never go to Germany. And she knew that Germany was my only chance for freedom.

In the meantime, I studied how to read and write Polish, so I could write Uncle Franek, Dieter, Ursula, Henryk, and my friend Renata. I wanted to be able to communicate with them even though Matka and I would be away in Germany.

When we finally received train tickets to Germany from the German government, I looked over them for hours. This was it. I was leaving the only home I had ever known. I would have to say goodbye to all my friends. My only comfort was that Matka was coming with me.

— — — — — — — — — — — —

The next day we got on the train with our two little bags — one for me and one for Matka. We sat close together and snuggled during the entire train ride. I enjoyed traveling with Matka. I felt so much safer with her than all those times I had traveled alone to the orphanages. We seemed to ride along forever, drifting in and out of sleep, lulled by the steady chug of the train slowly making its way through Poland.

We awoke when we came to an abrupt stop at the border of Poland and Germany. As we peered out the window, we could see soldiers surrounding the train. The soldiers' dogs were barking incessantly in the direction of one particular boxcar. A man jumped from beneath the boxcar, and a machine gun fired at him. His body dropped to the ground, lifeless. The authorities hardly hesitated. They gathered around the man and carried his limp body away from the tracks.

Shortly after they took away his body, the police boarded the train and asked everyone for their passports. I was frightened after hearing all the commotion outside. I didn't want to end up dead like that poor man. So I did as I was told and gave the policeman my passport and the other paperwork I had. He called over another policeman, and they looked over our documents.

"You cannot cross the border today," the policeman told us sternly.

"But, why not?" Matka cried out.

"This boy's name is spelled wrong. Is this a forged passport, madam? If so, you will be in severe trouble."

"No, we've had to change his paperwork in Warsaw so many times already. They told us everything was in order now."

"Clearly it is not. Please get off this train. You need to fix this before going farther."

Matka didn't put up a fight. Instead, we got off the train and found a trip back. Our long journey was a bust. But as we sat on the train to Toruń, I felt slightly relieved. Matka and I were going home.

_ _ _ _ _ _ _ _ _ _ _ _ _ _ _ _ _

A month later, we made the trip again and the same thing happened. The policemen once again collected our paperwork and told us we were unable to cross the border. So we returned home. This time, Matka made sure the documents were 100% correct.

I was 15 years old by the time the authorities finally let us cross — on our third trip to the Polish-German border. We were told to change trains as the police searched the boxcar. Soviet troops, East German troops, and Polish troops all stood around with machine guns, pistols, and dogs. There were even a couple of Soviet tanks sitting at the station. The whole scene was eerie. Even though there were Soviet and Polish soldiers in and around Toruń, I had never seen so many guns and tanks in my life.

As we crossed the border and began traveling through East Germany, we saw even more tanks and soldiers. Most of the buildings we saw along the way were bombed out. Nothing had been rebuilt since the war. At least in Poland there was some rebuilding going on. In East Germany, everything was destroyed. The only buildings that stood strong were giant apartment structures with thousands of windows. It seemed like a whole town could live in one building. The ugly structures jutted up out of the rubble as a haunting reflection of the communal living that embodied Communism. There was nothing unique about any of the giant apartment buildings. Everything looked the same: dreary and dull.

When we finally arrived in East Berlin, I surveyed the scene around me and felt nothing but despair. The entire city was destroyed. Every building was bombed out or falling apart. It reminded me of the other buildings I had seen so far in Germany, except I knew somehow that Berlin had been beautiful at one time. Instead of gorgeous structures surrounding the city, the bombed-out buildings sat in ruins. The clouds covered what little sun there was, and a gray dust seemed to have settled over the entire city. People scurried from one place to another without looking up or meeting the gaze of neighbors.

We waited in East Berlin for what seemed like hours as they went over our paperwork again. After some time, a couple of soldiers arrived and informed us that Matka and I had to be sent back to Poland. Some paperwork was missing or incorrect, and they weren't going to let us continue our journey. I didn't understand what they were saying or exactly why we had to be sent back, but we did what they told us. By this point, Matka and I were exhausted. We thought we were safe when we crossed the border, but apparently not. The Soviet Army's lack of organization when it came to paperwork was beginning to irritate me beyond measure, but we got back on the train and made our way to the border despite our frustrations.

When we returned to the Polish-German border, they made us get out of the train and asked us a round of questions. The Soviet soldiers first asked the name of my family in Germany. I didn't know the answer to that. Then they asked me about my father. Who was he, they hounded me. Again, I was unable to answer their questions. I explained that I didn't know; I was just a child. After hours of questioning, they finally realized I was telling everything I knew, so they allowed us to return to East Berlin.

We were so worn out that I didn't care if we ever reached West Berlin. I didn't care what the soldiers wanted or what opportunities I would receive in Germany. I didn't want to go. I wanted to go back to my friends and be with them. I missed them so much already. I didn't care if I had to live in another sewer system or even if I got beaten every day, as long as I could be back in Toruń with my friends. I missed our care-free adventures. I missed our plots of revenge and the laughter we shared. I even missed my town, walking along the Wisła River and climbing up old fortress walls. I missed our trips to visit the gypsies and the warm greetings Matka and I received when entering the camp. I just wanted to be home again.

We arrived in East Berlin for the second time and went through the same protocol we had gone through days before. As the soldiers went over our paperwork, they explained that it would be another two or three days before we could cross to West Berlin. The soldier was speaking German, so Matka had to explain it to me. The only languages I spoke were Polish and a little bit of Russian, but these German soldiers only understood German, Russian, and some English.

While we waited for the authorities to let us cross to West Berlin, Matka finally decided to tell me more about my birth mother and new family. In subsequent letters she received via the gypsies, she had come to find out the full story behind the photograph I had been given of the two girls. She tried to explain that they were my sisters, but I had trouble believing her. I told Matka that it couldn't be true, because those girls looked nothing like me. She insisted, however. She kept reiterating that I had a family beyond the people who loved me in Toruń. I had a family that loved me and wanted me.

"No, Matka!" I exclaimed. "I don't want that family. You are my family. You are my mother. You were there for me always. You are all I need."

She smiled and told me that she would always be my matka no matter what. She just wanted me to accept my new family as best as I could.

Within a day or so, the authorities told me that I was officially allowed to cross into West Berlin. Matka and I walked together toward a long line. An intimidating scene surrounded us. Soviet officers were stationed all around us with machine guns and tanks, and we were forced to walk between long lines of soldiers.

As I looked ahead into West Berlin, I noticed bombed-out buildings and barbed wire all over, but the streets seemed cleaner and more inviting. I didn't fully understand what I was seeing, because I had never been educated about the war. But I was wide-eyed with wonder as I counted the number of tanks, police, soldiers, and jeeps.

We arrived at a stopping point where we were informed that we were about to cross into West Berlin. I looked ahead and saw a big white line where we were to cross. My knees shook with fear. A soldier explained to Matka that I had to walk across this line with my hands on my head. Matka translated everything to me in detail. She ended with a solemn warning that if for any reason I were to turn around or start running, I would be shot on the spot. I was thoroughly petrified. I knew the soldiers would shoot me without even thinking about it.

"Piotr," Matka whispered to me, "Go. Don't look back. Just go."

I took a few steps forward, frightened like never before, holding my little bag of possessions tightly to my chest. This was my bag of treasures. Inside, I had my matka's picture, my sisters' picture, Henryk's picture, and something to remember all of my friends. Plus, I had a pair of shoes with holes in them and a pair of holey socks. All of these mementos were wrapped up nicely in a paper bag with a string, because we didn't have suitcases.

I stopped in my tracks, unsure of my own footing. I didn't feel right. I needed some kind of assurance that everything would be okay when I reached the other side.

I turned to Matka and said, "Matka, you have to walk with me. I'm too afraid to walk alone."

"No, Piotrusiu, you will have to walk first. That's what the soldiers say you must do."

I nodded, understanding that we had to abide by the rules of the soldiers. So I walked slowly ahead of Matka.

Matka didn't tell me the truth — she would not be crossing the line. I had assumed that she would be able to travel with me to West Berlin, but they wouldn't allow her to leave Communist control. She was forced to stay. The only reason she was allowed to leave Poland was to accompany me to East Berlin. As long as the Soviets were in power, she would never be able to cross into West Germany.

So I walked ahead, not knowing that this would be my last goodbye to my matka. Instead, I was consumed with the fear of doing something terribly wrong and being shot on the spot. I held my little bag of possessions in my hands above my head and made my way across the line. I looked straight forward, afraid to glance behind me or even to the side. I could see soldiers ahead of me. They looked different, though. They were German and American soldiers. And there were American tanks with big stars on them stationed across the line. When I finally made it to the other side, I breathed a sigh of relief and looked back toward Matka. I wanted to be sure she made it across safely, too.

When I turned and looked back, however, Matka was still standing on the other side. She was crying and waving to me.

In that moment, I realized she wasn't coming.

"Mamusiu! Mamusiu!" I screamed

All I could hear was her crying out to me, "*Dowezenia*, Piotrusiu! Goodbye, my son!"

"Mamusiu, Mamusiu!" I screamed again. "Come back! Come back!"

But she couldn't respond. A German officer had grabbed her by the arm and started walking her toward a waiting train.

I couldn't stand still and watch her walk away from me. How could I live my life without her? Without thinking, I started running. My eyes were blinded with tears. My only thought was to get to Matka before she left my sight. Before I could get very far, a soldier jumped toward me and grabbed me. I didn't understand what he said to me, but he was yelling. I didn't know what was happening; all I knew was that my heart was breaking into tiny pieces.

The soldier held on to me as I stood and watched Matka disappear into that same train we had arrived on days earlier. She was going back to Toruń without me.

I sobbed tears I didn't know I had. My heart felt as though it were nestled in the pit of my stomach. I wanted to vomit.

Matka was gone.

I felt betrayed and alone. I was in a place I didn't know, with people who didn't even speak my language. If there was ever a moment in my life when I despised everyone in the world, it was right then and there. I hated everyone. I had no desire to continue living.

I stood there motionless, holding my little bag of possessions. A man approached me and took me inside a little shack where they looked over my papers and stamped them. Several of the men inside the building tried to talk to me, but I didn't understand them. They shook my hand and smiled at me, but I didn't feel like smiling back. My world was over. I turned away and looked through the little window of the shack, hoping that Matka would somehow come back for me.

I loved that woman more than anything. She was the only family I had. She was my world, my life. The two of us had been through so much together, and we survived because we had each other. No one could understand what we went through together. The last thing I wanted was to be brought to my birth mother, a woman who had abandoned me as a baby. She was not my real mother, because she hadn't been there when I needed her most. Matka had been there for me, though. And I missed her terribly.

As I sat there thinking about Matka, I tried to devise ways that I could get back to her. I didn't know what to do. Should I try to run? Should I be shot and get it over with?

A policeman pulled me from these thoughts when he reached out for my hand. I followed him out of the shack and through a little walkway where there were more tanks and soldiers on duty. As I walked between the soldiers, I felt their eyes following me, but all I could do was weep for my loss.

———————————————

The policeman walked me toward a jeep with two black American soldiers standing nearby. They frightened me — I had never seen a black person before. The policeman handed them my papers and gave them my bag, which one of the soldiers put in the backseat for me. The policeman approached another American soldier and began speaking to him, leaving me to stand between the two black soldiers.

I thought I was going to hell. This was my final punishment, just as the nuns had told me long ago in the orphanage. I remembered the picture the crazy nun had shown me of the black devil with horns that took people to hell. As I looked up at the two men looming over me in their large helmets, I knew that this was my fate. This must be what was happening to me. And while I was frightened, I couldn't help but feel slightly relieved. Perhaps this meant my life would be over now. I wouldn't have to deal with any more sorrow and pain.

Fifteen minutes later, the policeman returned with all my papers in order, and the two men motioned for me to enter the jeep. I had never been in anything like a jeep before. I stared out the window in amazement as we drove through the busy city of Berlin. There were more cars than I had ever seen in my life. I felt like everyone was looking at me because I was in the jeep, but I didn't care. I didn't know where I was being taken or what was going to happen to me once I got there. I just wanted it to be over with already.

After a while, we stopped at a store within a big U.S. Army base. I had never seen so many people in one place before. There were all sorts of ethnicities and cultures represented — black people, white people, and even Asians. I didn't understand why they were all together. And there were so many things for them to buy. I really didn't understand how they could afford the carts and bags of food they were carrying out of the store. They had to be rich.

While we walked around the store, the two black soldiers picked out food and drink goodies. As we stood in line, I saw all the items people were buying and wished that my matka and my friends could have access to such large amounts of food. I decided that if I didn't go to hell right away, I would send them a package of food as soon as I could.

The three of us piled back into the jeep and made our way down the road. Eventually, we arrived at another checkpoint where we had to show our papers again. While we waited for permission to cross, we sat in a park and the two soldiers brought out their bag of goodies.

First, one of the soldiers pulled out bananas and offered me one. I had never seen a banana before, but I was hungry. The last time I had eaten was with Matka. I looked over the large yellow object and took a bite — without peeling it. It was rough and tasted disgusting. The two soldiers began laughing at me, nearly in hysterics. I knew they were trying to poison me. Why else would they be laughing?

The other soldier handed me an orange instead. I had never seen or tasted an orange either, so I did the same thing and tried to eat it peel and all. It was so bitter that I spit. Now I was angry. Why would they be teasing me this way? If they wanted to kill me, they should just shoot me and get it over with already.

"No, no, no!" one of the soldiers said to me in English, in between bouts of laughter. "This is how you do it."

Then he took the banana and showed me how to peel it. He took a bite to show me that it was edible, so I warily did the same. This time, it was good. So I ate another one and another one. In a matter of minutes, I had eaten all of the bananas. Then the soldier showed me how to peel an orange, so I ate that. It had an interesting taste, both sweet and sour. I ate about four. I probably could have eaten more, but they took too much patience to peel.

After our paperwork cleared, we were back on the road. While we rode along, one of the soldiers handed me a giant box of chocolates. I knew what chocolate was, so there were no misunderstandings about eating procedures. I was thrilled to be given my favorite treat. These men weren't devils after all. They were good people who were nice enough to feed me. I ate the whole box of chocolates in no time.

Within half an hour, however, my stomach began to hurt. Then it was absolutely going crazy. I tried communicating to the soldiers that I had to go to the bathroom right away, but they didn't understand me. They just laughed and talked in English. I tried explaining to them that I didn't feel good. I used hand gestures and everything, but they still didn't understand. I lay down in the back seat and tried to get comfortable, but my stomach was going glug, glug, glug, glug, glug.

All of a sudden, my stomach couldn't hold it in any longer. There was an explosion of diarrhea. Not only did I go all over myself, but I vomited as well. The soldiers finally realized what I had been trying to tell them. This time they tried to stop, but they couldn't because they could only pull over in designated areas.

Those poor soldiers had to ride with that smell and that vomit until the next rest area. They were gagging and laughing at the same time. They rolled up the flaps of the jeep and did their best to breathe by sticking their heads out the windows. It was January, so the cool, whipping wind had to have been sharp against their faces. I wasn't too concerned about their predicament, though, because my stomach was still doing flips.

When we finally pulled up to a rest area, they opened up the top and showed me where there was some water to clean myself off. Then they asked around for someone to give me a pair of pants to change into, so at least I was clean.

I was so sick that I ended up falling asleep for the rest of the trip.

Chapter 12

When we arrived at our final destination at a U.S. Army base, the two soldiers woke me up. I still felt completely nauseous and weak, drained from my sickness.

"Come on, kid. We're going to get you checked out," the soldier who had been sitting in the passenger seat said to me, motioning for me to come out of the jeep.

I did my best to inch out carefully and step onto the concrete below. I was covered in sweat, shivering as I stepped out into the frigid air. Even though it had been several hours since my "incident," my stomach was still gurgling.

I blinked my eyes a couple of times in the brightness of the sun and looked around. Everything seemed so foreign. The style of the buildings, the languages being spoken, and even the way people were dressed — everything was different from what I was used to in Poland.

"This way," said the other soldier, pointing at a building behind me.

I followed in step behind the soldiers as we climbed the large stairs to the building. The two soldiers held the door for me, and I made my way inside what I guessed was a hospital. There were children crying and adults sitting quietly in waiting areas. People in white coats scurried from room to room.

"Wait here," one of the soldiers said, pointing at a seat.

I was relieved to sit down, but soon I was being ushered into an exam room, where they poked and prodded me. The nurses drew a lot of blood and then asked me to take off my clothes. I hesitated for a moment, unsure what they wished to do to me. Such requests had always meant I would endure something horrible. Plus, I had been in more hospital rooms than I cared to remember. I didn't want to undergo any of the same tortures.

One of the nurses, sensing my uncertainty, approached me and gently coaxed me out of my pants and into a hospital gown. Then she had me lie down on my stomach, so they could put some white medicine on my behind. The cream stung horribly. I didn't quite understand why they seemed to be hurting me more than helping me, but the nurse seemed so kind and gentle that I figured there had to be a good reason.

After I was examined, I was taken to another room where some doctors showed me a card with a symbol or picture on it, and I was supposed to respond. I guess they were checking to see if I was normal. I must have passed inspection, because then they took me in another room and checked out my teeth, throat, and eyes.

After awhile, they settled me into a room with a couple of other people, but I had a section to myself. I lay in my little bed with the sheet pulled to my chin to keep out the cold.

"Some food for you, dear," a kind, elderly woman said as she placed before me a tray of delicious smelling food.

I tried to eat but could only swallow down a few bites. My stomach was still playing tricks on me.

"Here, darling, take this to help settle your stomach," the woman said as she held out a white pill.

Like every other conversation at the hospital, I didn't understand what she was saying to me. But I could tell that she wanted me to swallow the white pill she had placed in my hand. I put it in my mouth and took a swig of water to gulp it down.

"Good. You'll begin to feel better soon, I promise," she told me as she left the room.

By that point, I was exhausted. Not only had I traveled from Poland to Germany, but I had crossed the Communist border as well. All the stress of traveling finally hit me, so I allowed myself to fully relax, snuggling into my comfortable bed. Within a few minutes, I fell into a deep sleep.

————————————————

When I awoke, I wasn't alone. A middle-aged woman sat at the foot of my bed.

"*Dzien dobre*, Piotr! How are you feeling?" the woman asked.

It took me a moment to realize that I understood what she was saying.

"Better. My stomach isn't gurgling as much. You speak Polish?" I asked excitedly, no longer worried about my health.

"A little bit. The doctors sent me down here so that I could talk to you. I know you've felt alone and confused here. Do you understand why you are here?"

I shrugged my shoulders.

"Well, you're in this hospital because you are dehydrated. The two officers that brought you here from Berlin told us that you were ill, so we had you checked out. We can tell you haven't eaten much, because you're underweight for your age. You poor thing! You're just skin and bones. But the doctors here will get you better, so you can keep your food and drink in your belly!"

I nodded in understanding.

"But, you are really here at this base because your mother is here. She's been waiting for you for a long time now. And after you are made well, you'll be able to go and see her! Isn't that exciting?" she asked, smiling.

"No," I responded, baffling the woman completely. "I don't want to see my birth mother. I already have a mother in Poland. She is my real mother. We love each other, and I miss her…"

I broke into tears. I couldn't hold them in any longer.

"Oh, Piotr!" she cried, holding out her arms to me. "I know you miss your matka in Poland, but think about your mother here. She has been missing you for over ten years!"

"I don't care," I sobbed. "She doesn't love me. If she loved me, she would never have abandoned me! I hate her! I hate her! I hope she goes to live in hell with the devil. She's not my mother!"

The woman didn't say anything in response. She just held me in her arms and rocked me. I felt tears fall from her face onto my head. She felt my pain, even if she didn't fully understand it.

After I calmed down a bit, she let go of me and looked me in the eyes.

"Piotr, you are here now. You have a new life with a new family. You will never lose the love of your matka. She will always love you. You must understand, though, that you are German. You belong here in Germany."

"I am not German," I interrupted. "I'm Polish!"

"No, Piotr, you are a German," she responded firmly.

"How can that be? I grew up in Poland. I speak Polish. My matka is Polish. How can I be German?" I asked, confused.

"Your birth mother is German, so you are German. When you meet her, she'll explain the rest. It's not for me to explain what happened. Only your mother can do that."

And we left the conversation there. She knew that she wouldn't be able to get through to me. The anger I held against my birth mother was too great. I cursed her name. I cursed her family. I cursed the day that I was born to her. I wanted my matka in Poland. Why couldn't I have been her real son? Why was my life so messed up?

— — — — — — — — — — — — — — — — —

A few days later I was released from the hospital. The soldiers who picked me up gave me a new pair of pants, a shirt, and some shoes. I was cleaned up and looking better than I had in quite some time. They drove me to a little building and led me to a small room.

The room was really cozy. There were two small twin beds situated side by side, as well as a couple of sitting chairs and couches. The radio was turned on and playing a happy tune that reminded me a bit of my evenings at the gypsy camp. There was even a television in the room.

What really got my attention was the large bowl of fruit on the table. There were so many different kinds of fruit, some of which I had never seen before. I noticed the oranges and bananas first, but I stayed away from those. Instead, I was drawn to the apples, pears, and plums. I didn't take one, though. I didn't want to risk getting sick again.

As I continued to survey the room, I noticed a woman for the first time, sitting silently on a stiff-backed chair in the corner of the room. She stood up, her eyes overflowing with tears. She didn't move toward me, nor did I move toward her.

I knew who she was immediately, but my heart was hardened. The hatred I felt for my mother filled me to the brim. As we stood there looking at each other, she took a step to come closer to me. I immediately backed away, causing her to stop.

I looked her in the eyes with as much hatred as I could muster, but she just stood there weeping before me. She tried speaking to me, but she didn't speak Polish. She could only speak German and English. I didn't know what she was saying, but she kept chanting over and over again, "*Mein leiber Peter, mein leiber Peter.*"

We stood there for some time, not moving forward and not moving backward. She sobbed and I stood bitterly. Then, not knowing how else to communicate with me, she began to take off some of her clothes, pointing out scars on her arms, including a row of numbers tattooed on her forearm. I hardly had time to take it all in when she opened her shirt and showed me her mutilated breasts. They were scarred and hanging loosely.

And as she showed me the painful scars, I realized that she had suffered as much as I had. I didn't understand what had happened to her or why she looked the way she did, but in that particular moment, a little of my hatred began to melt away.

I looked her in the eyes and saw that she was still crying. I realized that tears were falling from my eyes, too. As more of my bitterness began to melt away, my mother took me in her arms and embraced me. We held each other and cried for some time. She kissed my face and my hands, and I let her. I wanted to feel the touch of my mother. I realized for the first time that I did love her. I didn't love her like my matka nor did I trust her, but I was beginning to understand what it might have been like to have a "real" mother.

I don't know how long we held each other and cried, but eventually we fell asleep. I hadn't anticipated such an emotionally draining reunion.

— — — — — — — — — — — — — — —

When I awoke the next morning, my mother was already awake, sitting in a chair, watching me. She smiled. I wasn't exactly sure how to respond. The night before had me so confused. I didn't know how I felt. After all, my birth mother was a complete stranger to me. I still had so many questions that needed answering.

After eating a light breakfast in awkward silence, the two of us went on a walk together. We walked for hours, not talking because we didn't speak the same language, but we were together. The awkwardness began to fade as we spent time together, and when she grabbed my hand, I let her, enjoying the touch of my mother.

We walked up and down the streets, looking at the little homes and shops in and around the base. The weather was cold, causing me to pull my hands up into the sleeves of my little coat. The wind swept through my hair, messing it up slightly. My mother reached out and moved her hand through my hair. I looked up at her and smiled, which brought her to tears. She stood over me, both hands clasping my face, and kissed me on the forehead.

Then she pointed to a small café on the corner of the street. We made our way inside and sat down. My mother motioned toward a table, full of all sorts of meat, fruit, and bread. I piled my plate to the brim and got up for seconds and thirds. I had never seen so much food in my life. I was in heaven.

After walking for a few more hours, we stopped in another little store for some dessert. My mother allowed me to buy a huge bowl full of ice cream. It was freezing outside, but I didn't care. I had never tasted anything so delicious.

My first day with my mother was quickly becoming one of the best days of my life. I only wished my matka and friends could have enjoyed the tastes of those foods with me. And while I missed them all, I had to admit that I was enjoying my time with my mother.

— — — — — — — — — — — — — — — —

When we finally returned to our little room, my mother began speaking to me in German, trying to tell me something of importance. I just nodded my head. Not being able to communicate with her was definitely a problem. As much fun as we had just being together, I still had so many questions to ask. I still wanted to know why she had abandoned me and why she wanted me now, after all of these years. Nothing made sense.

Those questions had to wait until another time, however, because at that very moment two young girls entered the room. I knew right away that these were my sisters, because I recognized them from the picture I received back in Poland.

As I watched them approach their mother and eye me suspiciously, I couldn't help but think how different they were from me. Their skin was a light brown, an obvious contrast to my pasty white skin. The older of the little girls, about six years old, had kinky blonde hair. The younger one, about four years old, had kinky brown hair. I had never seen such tight curls in my life. Though they had darker skin than me and my mother, they were lighter than the two black soldiers who had driven me to the base. I was continually amazed by the variety of people and cultures I encountered in Germany.

The three of us stared at each other for quite some time before I decided to kneel down to their level. They were shy, I could tell, but they were so cute. As I knelt down, they approached me, and I embraced them with a hug. I held them tightly, breathing in their fresh innocence. They didn't seem so afraid of me any more and hugged me back. After letting them go, the three of us were no longer strangers. They began chattering away, trying to tell me their life stories. They pointed and tugged on me, asking me questions in a language I didn't understand. I laughed, though, because they were obviously quite excited. They certainly weren't shy anymore.

After trying to communicate verbally for a while, we began communicating through hand signals, which worked much better. They sat on my lap and showed me their toys one by one. We played with each of them, laughing and making faces the entire time. I had never had a brother or a sister before. I didn't know what having siblings felt like. Henryk had brothers, which I envied at times, but for the most part everyone I knew was an only child. And though the three of us couldn't verbally communicate, I knew in that moment that I had a real family. Those girls meant everything to me. I had just met them, but I would protect them to the end of time. They were my flesh and blood. And they were absolutely beautiful. I never felt so proud.

My mother watched us for awhile, before finally motioning for us to come outside with her. The four of us walked to a nearby park. Both girls immediately ran for the swings, so I got behind them and pushed them both up and down. They squealed and laughed in delight. Barbara, the younger of the two, was a daredevil and jumped from the swing and began running toward a lake not too far away. Georgia followed suit, while my mother and I ran after them.

The two girls ran along the edge of lake, splashing up chunks of ice. I followed closely behind them and put my cold hands on the back of Barbara's neck. She squealed and splashed me with the freezing water. I laughed, enjoying the fun. I noticed that my mother had sat down underneath a tree, watching us. She seemed to have faded into the background as the three of us played together, but every once in awhile I would look up and find her smiling at us through tears of joy.

After hours of playing, we finally bundled back up and headed home for supper. We had calmed down some, but we still laughed and showed off our funny faces. Although we didn't speak the same language, somehow we were able to express ourselves without words. We were a family. And it actually felt good.

— — — — — — — — — — — — — — —

Our tight-knit family of four didn't last long, however. A couple of days later I met my stepfather, George — a tall, African-American soldier. He put my hand in his and shook it with little enthusiasm. There was no warmth or embrace from him, just a cold greeting. He tried to say something in English, but it was lost on me.

I was scared. Aside from the gypsy king, who came and went with the seasons, I had never had a real male figure in my life. My matka was never married. I didn't really know what it was like to have a father or how I should behave in front of a father. Plus, George was an American soldier. Having never met an American (aside from the soldiers who brought me on base), I didn't know how to act. I knew that being an American must be thrilling. He must have had countless adventures living in his vast homeland. I was in complete awe of him.

A few days after George arrived, an officer picked us up and drove us to my family's real home at the Army base in Baumholder, Germany. As we traveled there, I couldn't help but remember the last trip I made with Matka. I missed her so much. My mother sat in the backseat with me caressing my hand, but I wanted my matka with me instead. I wondered what she was doing and if she missed me, too. I had sent her a letter, but I hadn't received a response yet.

The girls tried to play with me, but I wasn't really in the mood. I missed home too much. I tried to laugh every once in awhile to show that I wasn't angry with them, but inside I was crying for Poland. I was so homesick.

When we arrived at their home, I knew I didn't belong. They lived in an apartment building with all sorts of neighbors. As we made our way up to their apartment, I could sense some sort of tension. Right away people seemed to be looking at us differently, treating us differently. The neighbors stared just a little too long.

But perhaps I was just being overly suspicious due to my homesickness and my past experiences of not being accepted. Plus, I was tired. After showing me around their home and having a small bite to eat, my mother and sisters finally showed me where I would be sleeping.

They took me to a small room with three little beds. The girls were to sleep in a bunk bed, while I would sleep in a tiny bed beside them. My mother tucked the girls in, kissing them each on the forehead, before approaching my bedside. She sat on the edge of my bed, leaned in and kissed me as well. She quietly tip-toed out of the room, shutting the door behind her.

My mind drifted back to Poland as I fell asleep. Even though life wasn't always good there, I felt I was moving too fast here. I couldn't catch my breath. Every day was something new. And half the time I didn't understand what was going on around me. I slept peacefully that night, however, as I dreamt of Matka in our little home in Poland.

A sharp pain awoke me from my sleep. Someone or something had poked me hard in the eye. As I jumped up from my bed, my sisters ran in opposite directions, shrieking. They had pulled up my eyelids and thrust their fingers in my eye to wake me up. Once I calmed down from my rude awakening, I couldn't help but laugh. They were more like me than I had realized. A mischievous streak definitely ran through our blood line. Perhaps I did belong here after all.

Chapter 13

After a week or two of living with my new family, I came home one day from playing with my sisters and found my mother sitting at the kitchen table looking at a map. She smiled as I came in the door and motioned for me to sit down next to her.

She had circled several cities on a large map of Germany. One by one, she pointed to each of the circled cities. Then she took me by the hand and led me to my bedroom. Sitting on my bed was a little suitcase packed with a few shirts and pants that my stepfather had recently bought me at the PX, the store located on the base. Apparently we were going on a trip.

My mother and I left early the next morning before my sisters were even awake. The drive with Mama was much more relaxed than my trip with the two soldiers from Berlin. I was able to take in the scenery and enjoy a sense of peace.

I looked out the window and saw the Rhine River. The river was moving despite bits of floating ice. Sunlight bounced off its surface, casting rays of gold on the banks. It reminded me of the Wisła River back home. I could see buildings and homes lining the river. We were clearly near a city.

"Köln," Mama said from the driver seat. I remembered seeing it on the map she had shown me.

After driving down some winding streets within the city, my mother finally pulled the car to the side and parked. She looked at me, tears welling up in her eyes. I didn't know where we were going, but I could sense her hesitation. Her hand trembled as she grabbed the door handle. I reached over and patted her on the shoulder. I wanted her to know I was with her, even though I didn't know what we were up against. She smiled at me, taking my hand and kissing it.

We made our way to a house down the block. Mama paused slightly before knocking. When she did, I could feel her tense up. We waited a moment before a man opened the door.

He was evidently shocked to see us standing on his doorstep. The look on his face said as much. He was middle-aged, probably a little younger than my mother, and by the way he was dressed I guessed he was pretty well-off.

After overcoming his shock, his manners kicked in and he cordially invited us in out of the cold. But his friendliness was a thin façade. His shock seemed to have given way to muted displeasure. As I looked him over, I could see a resemblance between him and Mama.

I stood to the side as Mama and the man made their formal greetings. I heard her call him *bruder*, a German word that I recognized. Georgia and Barbara used it when they spoke of me to their friends. Until that moment, I didn't even know that my mother had any siblings. But evidently I had an uncle.

The two exchanged words for a few minutes before their attention turned to me. The man looked me up and down, appraising me, before giving me his hand to shake. Then he turned and led us into the sitting room.

Neither he nor Mama looked happy. The man would barely look at me. As if the bitter undertones in his voice weren't enough, his face communicated his displeasure. He wasn't happy to see either of us. And I couldn't help but feel it had something to do with me.

As the two sat and talked in German, I nibbled on some cookies and observed the room where we were sitting. My eyes kept wandering to the back wall. On it was a plaque with the word "FORD" in big letters. I remembered my mother mentioning the word to me as we drove to Köln. She must have been referring to my uncle, since it was evident that he worked for the Ford Motor Company in Germany.

Clearly my uncle was proud of his achievements at the company, and his sterile floors and finely furnished home indicated that he was doing well financially. Perhaps that was why he didn't enjoy our visit — perhaps he was embarrassed by our lack of prestige. Or worse yet, perhaps he thought we were there for a hand-out.

We sat together for an hour or so before my uncle's wife arrived home. She appeared even more surprised to see the two of us than her husband had. She looked like she had stepped right out of an advertisement. Her hair was tied back nicely in a well-manicured style, which framed her face favorably. But there was a kindness about her, and I could tell she was genuine when she smiled at Mama and at me. She patted me on the head and said something in German that made my mother smile.

Though my aunt seemed pleased by our visit, I sensed that our presence wasn't a comfortable situation for my uncle. He sat rigidly with his arms crossed, tapping his foot to a steady beat as though irritated. A sense of relief swept across his face when Mama finally mentioned that we should get going. He gave her a quick, tense hug and a kiss on the cheek. Then he shook my hand again, and we left.

Instead of going directly back to our car, Mama and I walked around the city a bit. She wanted to show me the Rhine River up close. As we walked toward it, a gothic-looking cathedral loomed up ahead. It was immense, like nothing I had ever seen. I could even see gargoyles up on top. We passed by the cathedral and walked across a bridge, so we could look down into the waters of the Rhine below. The wind was blowing hard, but it didn't seem to bother my mother much. She simply stared across the river, her mind elsewhere.

I wondered what she might have shared with me had we spoken the same language — would she have explained why her brother was so distant? Maybe she would have told me why we were making this particular journey together. Perhaps she could have even told me why she had abandoned me as a baby. So much could have been said, but instead we each remained isolated in our own troubled thoughts.

After a few minutes she snapped out of it, and we walked back to the car. This time, we were headed for Dortmund.

———————————————

In Dortmund, my mother didn't seem nearly as nervous as she had when we visited her brother. She knocked on the door of a small flat and called out that it was she, Helena. A woman's voice could be heard on the other side, asking another question. My mother responded in turn, and then we stood outside for several more minutes as the woman unlocked each lock on her door. She must have had at least seven locks. We heard each one — click, click, click, click — before she opened the door.

When I walked into the apartment, my first reaction was that something must have happened to this poor woman. The house was like a cave, all dark and musty. And the poor woman's body was shriveled and crunched up. Her body looked ancient, but I could tell from her face that she couldn't have been much older than my mother.

Mama hugged and kissed the wretched-looking woman before looking at me and saying something to her in German about me.

The woman's response surprised me. Tears began streaming down her face. She began sobbing like Mama had sobbed the first time we met in that little room. Then she rushed toward me and started touching my face and my hands. She kissed my hands, my head, and then my cheeks. I didn't know who the woman was or why she was so pleased to see me, but it felt good to be well received.

My mother and I stayed with the woman for a day or two. While we were there, I tried to piece together who she was. My first clue came from the German words that I was beginning to recognize. Then the woman showed me pictures of my mother, herself, my uncle, and another man and woman, presumably their parents. It made sense that the two were sisters. They seemed so close.

At the same time, the two seemed so different. My mother had shown me her scars the first day we met, so I knew something terrible had happened to her. But my auntie seemed scarred mentally and emotionally, too. Every time we left the house, she painstakingly locked each lock. And even when things seemed to be going well and she and Mama were laughing, she would suddenly burst into tears. When such moments occurred, my mother would do her best to comfort her. Often Mama would call me over to comfort her as well. I seemed to help, because my auntie would hold me tightly, rock me, and kiss my hands. I didn't know what had happened to her, but I knew that she loved me and that felt good.

When Mama said it was time for us to continue on with our trip, my auntie burst into tears once again. Mama assured her that we would be back to see her some time soon. But I never saw my auntie again.

— — — — — — — — — — — — — — — — —

Our next stop was a town near Lubeck, Germany. The neighborhood where we parked seemed peaceful enough, but I could already sense tension in the air. My mother looked more determined than nervous when she knocked on the door of a house on the corner. I saw a young girl peer out the window, and then another set of eyes appeared. Swiftly, the door opened and two women stood before us looking even more adamant than Mama.

My mother and the older of the two women stared at each other for a moment before Mama explained the reason for our visit.

"This is my son," Mama began, but she hardly had a chance to complete her sentence when the woman began screaming at her.

I didn't understand what the woman was screaming, but I watched intently as my mother became very animated, pointing to me with both of her hands, yelling something about how "he belongs to you!" I didn't understand everything, but I caught that much.

The woman laughed in spite and spat on the doorstep. Then she cursed us in German. She obviously wanted nothing to do with me or my mother.

"You are both dirty Jews! Get out of my face. Get out of my yard. You are not family! Even your own father despised you. Jew blood runs thick, and we don't want any of that here!"

Mama stopped in her tracks and immediately broke down in tears. I didn't know what this woman meant by calling us Jews. It didn't make sense to me at all, but I felt compassion for my mother. I hated being called hurtful names, just as she must.

Mama grabbed my hand and ran back to the car. I looked at the two women behind me and saw smug looks of satisfaction cross their faces. I hated them both.

Later I learned that one of the women on the doorstep was actually my step-grandmother. She had married my mother's father during the war (after my grandmother was murdered for being a German Jew).

Mama barely said a word as we drove off. She wiped away the tears and stared straight down the road. We didn't stop until we got to Hanover. Once there, we stayed with some friends of my mother's. They were very kind and embraced me right away. I learned that they were Jewish people. Perhaps this was what that woman had been referring to earlier; perhaps she didn't like the fact that my mother had Jewish friends. I found nothing wrong with them, though. Aside from my auntie, they were the kindest people we met on the trip.

——————————————————

When my mother and I finally returned home to Baumholder, my sisters met us at the door with hugs and kisses. Even George looked happy to see that we had returned safely.

After we arrived home, I realized that I hadn't thought of Poland during our entire trip. I couldn't believe it had slipped my mind. I had such an enjoyable time with my mother that I forgot to miss my real home.

But once I recognized my lapse, all those thoughts and feelings came rushing back to me. I started thinking about my matka and my friends. I loved my matka so much. I didn't think it was possible to miss her as much as I did.

Time passed quickly, though, and while I didn't forget my matka and friends in Poland, I had begun a new life in Germany. My new family and I traveled to different places and saw new and exciting things. In the fall, we drove to Austria and France. The different countries were so beautiful. What made it better was that I never had to worry about my identification papers when we crossed the borders. My new papers, which I had received right before moving to Baumholder, stated that I was German. I even had a German passport.

I was so proud of my passport. It was green with a black eagle on the front cover. And it stated in black and white that I was German. Of course, I could barely speak the German language, but according to my documents I was a German citizen. So when we crossed the border, they just stamped my passport and I was free to go as I pleased.

After our trip to Austria, we drove to Frankfurt, Germany. George explained that we were going there to visit the United States Embassy. As we drove into the city, there were cars, jeeps, and military trucks everywhere. It reminded me of Berlin, except much bigger. There was still a little damage from the war, but most of it had been rebuilt already.

Being in such a large city was exciting, particularly because there were so many different people in one place. Everywhere we turned there were different types of soldiers on duty. I saw French troops, British troops and American troops. And of course, there were German troops swarming in and out of the crowds of people, wearing tall, white hats. I could hardly tear my eyes away from them.

My attention shifted when we arrived at the U.S. Embassy. Standing guard were two military men wearing helmets and brightly colored uniforms, pressed to perfection. I noticed the shiny black pistols they carried at their sides, secretly wishing I owned one too. They saluted us immediately when they saw George in his army uniform. I felt so proud when I walked in the building. The embassy represented my stepfather's home, but to me it stood for so much more. It represented freedom and opportunity.

We stood in a long line awaiting the necessary documents that would allow me to travel more extensively with my family. My mother filled out the paperwork for me, because I didn't understand what needed to be written. This much I did understand — in a short time, the five of us would be leaving Germany to live in the United States.

While I was absolutely thrilled at the prospect of leaving Europe to live in the United States, I couldn't help but feel a pang of sorrow.

If I left Germany for the United States, I would be even farther away from my matka in Poland. My heart still felt torn in two — torn between the world I had grown up in and loved and this new world I was now discovering.

———————————————

When we got back to Baumholder, I had to start attending school so that I could learn English and German. I knew I had to learn something if I was ever going to survive in Germany or in the United States. School was rough, though. I was always being called a "dumb Pollock." Everyone made fun of me, because I didn't know how to speak correctly.

Even when I would go to the store and ask for something in German, the store clerk would hear my accent and call me a "dumb Pollock." I knew I wasn't stupid. It seemed like everyone in Germany believed that all Polish people were stupid. But they had never met my matka. She was brilliant. If they had met her, they would have changed their tunes.

If I responded that I was German, not Polish, my classmates would laugh at me. I even showed them my German passport once, but they continued to make fun of me and told me that I wasn't a "real" German. All the teasing made me remember my experiences in Poland and the taunting at the orphanages. To the Poles, I was a German; to the Germans, I was a Pole. I couldn't win.

Who was I, anyway? I didn't know. Poland was my home. My real family and friends were there. But there wasn't an ounce of Polish blood running through my veins. Biologically I had German blood, yet I knew nothing about Germany or its people.

Still, I felt compelled to call myself a German. Perhaps it was because I wanted to be liked; I wanted to fit in, if I could. And being Polish was definitely not the path to social acceptance in post-war Germany.

My mother saw the trouble I was going through at school, so she tried to embrace me with love. But even when I was with her, I felt the sting of outsiders' glares. When we would walk as a family through the streets, people always turned and stared at us. Sometimes people would actually point fingers at us and call my sisters foul names.

I began to really dislike the world I was living in. I didn't like Germany or the German people. They were no different from the Polish people who had called me names. What I hated most was when those fingers and name-calling were directed at my sisters. I knew what it felt like to be hated and disliked. I didn't want my little sisters to go through the same thing I did. I couldn't wait to get out of Germany. The more talk I heard of moving to America, the more excited I became.

When I finally received the news that my visa had been approved, my family and I celebrated with a big dinner. The United States wanted me. And we were all going to live happily ever after, just like I remembered seeing in the movies. The good cowboys always rode off into the sunset happy as can be. That was what would happen for me when we arrived in the United States. I couldn't wait.

That night, I offered to give the girls a bath while Mama and George celebrated with some wine. The girls got in the bathtub, and I ran some warm water and threw in a bunch of soap. As I looked at their dark skin, I couldn't help but think about the names some of the other kids called my sisters. Each time they teased one of my sisters, they always said something about the color of their skin. I thought that perhaps if I was able to scrub away some of the darkness, they wouldn't be teased as much.

I came up with the best idea. I ran to the cabinet and grabbed some Comet. I had seen my mother scrub the sink with it and noticed that it easily wiped away all the grease and dark areas. So I poured some of the white powder onto a wet washcloth and grabbed a hold of Georgia's arm, scrubbing away.

I never heard a child scream so loud in my life. I tried to explain that it would help her. If I could just wipe off the darkness, people would leave her alone. She didn't understand me, of course, because I was speaking excitedly in Polish. When she realized I wasn't stopping, she screamed even louder.

I let go of her arm and reached out for Barbara. She was the darker of the two anyway, so I figured it would probably help her out even more than Georgia. I hardly touched her, and she began to cry, probably due to the high-pitched screams of her sister.

My mother and George ran in within seconds of Barbara's painful cry.

"What are you doing?" George thundered at me.

I pointed to the Comet and Barbara's skin and tried my best to explain in broken German why I had wanted to scrub the darkness from their bodies.

"No, no!" my mother told me firmly, though seeming to understand why I had done such a thing.

She grabbed poor Georgia out of the tub, wrapping a towel around her shivering body. She rocked her back and forth, trying to comfort her. George did the same for Barbara, but his eyes pierced mine with anger.

I loved my sisters and never wanted to hurt them. I just didn't want them to suffer the emotional pain that I had endured. I thought that I could wipe away the darkness of their skin, therefore wiping away any chance of being teased. Apparently, I was wrong. And I felt horrible for having hurt them even more. Just like me, they were different from everyone else, and they were going to have to learn how to handle the rejection. I wondered why life was so cruel.

— — — — — — — — — — — — — — — —

Within a few days all was forgiven, and my sisters realized that I hadn't set out to harm them. They were back to sticking their fingers in my eyes when I slept and pulling my hair whenever they got the chance. The teasing at school hadn't subsided, but at least we were a family that stuck together.

Plus, it was September 2, 1959, my sixteenth birthday. The girls and I loitered around the house for a while before Mama told us to go outside and play for a couple of hours. I didn't mind; the girls and I always had more fun together when we could run around. But I did my best to avoid other children, so my sisters wouldn't have to deal with any taunting.

Georgia led the way, straight to the park. My sisters knew how to tire me out, but they were worth it. They always had me laughing or running after them in some game they made up. Or maybe it was a real game, but they always changed the rules on me. I never knew what was going on at the moment, so I just did my best to keep up with them.

After a couple of hours of intense playing, we called it a day and headed back to the apartment. As we climbed up our stairs, we counted each step. Georgia counted in German, Barbara counted in English, and I counted in Polish. We were learning and teaching at the same time. When we reached the landing at the top we all jumped at the same time, trying to yell loudest in our language. We laughed hard, because none of us could tell who won.

When we opened the door of our apartment and walked into the front hallway, I immediately smelled something delicious.

"Surprise!"

People from every nook and cranny of our tiny apartment jumped out of their hiding places and clapped their hands in my direction. I was shocked.

"Happy Birthday, Peter!" my mother said, smiling.

I was stunned. I had never had a birthday party before — unless you counted the time I went to the gypsy camp on my fourteenth birthday only to find out that my matka was not really my mother at all. Not a happy day by any means.

This was different. There was a cake sitting on the kitchen table with a bunch of candles sticking up out of it. And there were packages lined along the counter, all wrapped up and with my name on them. Plus, Mama's friends and some neighbors who had befriended us were there to celebrate with me.

My mother told me to blow out the candles while everyone sang me a song. I had never had a birthday cake with candles on it. When I blew them out, everyone clapped. I was ecstatic.

Then, one by one, people began handing me birthday presents to open. I didn't even know people received presents on their birthdays, but I sure wasn't complaining. The first gift I opened was a 45 rpm record player. Next, I opened up a bunch of records. One of them was Bill Haley. I loved his rock and roll music. I had never felt happier in my life.

Georgia and Barbara helped me open the rest of my presents, each one special to my heart. I received checkered shirts and pants. One of the neighbors bought me a BB gun. I even got cowboy boots. I was so happy, because I had a whole cowboy outfit and even some western songs on my records. I was going to be a real cowboy in the United States.

Life was pretty good. As I looked at all the gifts on the table before me, I had never felt more grateful. I only wished that my matka could celebrate with me. Her presence would be the greatest present of all.

I had written Matka so many letters, but I never got any sort of communication back. I knew that part of the reason had to do with the Communist government in Poland, but I still feared that something might have happened to Matka after she left me in Berlin. I wrote her every week, telling her about my sisters and school. I told her how I was still being teased and how I missed her and our little home in Toruń. I told her that even though things were okay here, I would rather be back with her in Poland. I ran to the mailbox every day to see if there was a letter for me, but I always came away empty-handed and broken-hearted.

— — — — — — — — — — — — — — —

A day or two after my birthday, my mother told me that I had a telephone call. I couldn't imagine who might be calling me, because I didn't have any friends at school. I was excited, though, because I hardly ever got the chance to use the telephone.

"Hello?" I said into the line.

"*Cześć*, Piotr," said the voice of my matka on the other end.

I nearly dropped the telephone. I hadn't expected to hear her voice. I knew that Matka didn't have a telephone. The only telephone she had access to was in the post office located in our town square.

"Mamusiu, did you get my letters?" I asked.

"Yes, Piotr, and your packages too. Did you get my letter to you?" she asked.

"No!" I cried, tears already rolling down my cheeks. "Mamusiu, I miss you. Please, can I come back home to you?"

I could hear muffled cries on her end of the line.

"How is your new family? Are they treating you well?" she asked, avoiding my question.

"Yes, they treat me good. But Mamusiu, I love you and want to be with you instead. Why can't I just live with you?"

"You need to be with your new family. Your real mama loves you. She needs to have the time she has lost to spend with you. She deserves that much, Piotr. You must be good and kind to her. She has been through much," Matka said.

"She is kind, but Matka, she isn't you. I love you more. You are my real mother!"

My tears were coming down faster now. I had to wipe my nose with the back of my sleeve. I didn't care that I looked a mess. My matka was on the other line. She was alive and okay. But, she was still so far away.

"Mamusiu, I love you," I said again.

"I love you, too."

We stated those same words over and over again. It was all I could think of saying. There were no other words to express how I was feeling.

"Are you happy, Piotr?" she finally asked.

"No, Matka, I want to come home."

"You know you can't."

"You don't understand, though!" I cried out. "I will be leaving for the United States in a few days! I don't know if I will ever see you again! Please, Matka. I have to see you again!"

"Oh, Piotr! Your life will be so much better in America. Just write me lots and lots of letters. And send me lots of pictures of you. You may not be able to see me, but I am with you always. You are always in my thoughts. And I know God is protecting you wherever you go. I never stop thinking of you, my Piotr. You are my only son. And I love you..." her voice broke off.

"I love you, too, Mamusiu..."

173

The line was cut off and an operator's voice came over the telephone. She said something in German, and then all I could hear was silence.

I hung up the phone, sobbing uncontrollably. I ran into my room and flopped onto my bed, burying my head in my pillow. I was overjoyed at having been able to speak to my matka, but I felt worse than I had in a long time. The ache in my heart was almost too much to bear. The only woman who had ever unconditionally cared for me was living in a country that didn't want me. Even if I could somehow see my matka, I would never be allowed to cross over the Polish border. I was told that I would never be able to return to Poland again. The finality of those words made me wish I were dead.

"Why, God, do you hate me so much?" I cried out as loud as I could.

There was no answer.

My matka had explained to me when I was a child about this man named Jesus and how He was the Son of God who came to take away the sins of the world. I saw Him pierced and hanging from the cross and could sympathize with the pain He must have endured. But if this God was supposed to love and care for me as much as she said He did, then why would He condemn me to endure so much? I could feel anger and bitterness begin to grow inside of me. I was angry at this God, and I was angry at everyone around me. I couldn't trust anyone, not even God.

How could anybody understand what I was going through? I had no one to talk to; I had no one to explain how I was feeling or what pain I was suffering. The only thing I could do was physically reach out to the sky and cry. I didn't know who or what I was reaching for, I just knew that I needed to grab hold of something. I was torn between two mothers. Two nations. Two worlds. Who was I? What really happened to me?

I knew that I had suffered about as much as I could physically bear in the orphanages of Poland. I understood now that the beatings I went through were because I was German or because of something my father had done. Although I wasn't being physically beaten in Germany, I felt like I was going through the same turmoil emotionally. As I contemplated my past, I resigned myself to accept suffering as my fate. My life seemed destined for difficulty, so I might as well get used to it.

On the other hand, as much as I had developed a hatred toward everyone around me, I had truly grown to love my sisters and my new mother. Yet at the same time we really couldn't communicate with one another.

Everything was just going too fast. I couldn't learn quickly enough. I couldn't understand what was going on half the time or why I was even in Germany. I still didn't know why my mother had abandoned me when I was a baby. None of my questions had been answered. I felt so confused. And it seemed as though no one cared enough to take the time to teach me.

The only thing that kept me from falling into the depths of depression was the fact that my matka loved me. She was always thinking of me. Though she wasn't physically with me, she was praying to her God for me. If her God didn't answer my prayers, then perhaps He would answer hers. And maybe she was right. Maybe when we went to the United States, life would get better for me. After all, I had all my cowboy stuff packed and ready to go. In two days we were leaving Germany. Could the pain I'd been living with finally be over with?

I could only hope.

Chapter 14

On September 6, 1959, my family and I finally left Germany for the United States. I looked out the window of the TWA plane as we approached the United States, and all I could see were buildings on either side of us. They started out small, but they quickly grew taller and more massive than I could have ever imagined. This was the New York City I had seen in the movies they showed at the American base. The city where dreams became reality.

"Welcome to America!" the flight attendant greeted us as we came to our final stop. Although I knew very little English, I did understand what she said. America! We had arrived at last.

The aisles of the plane were crowded with everyone trying to stretch after the long flight. As people started moving, I began to feel the excitement of being in America. But the line out of the plane was so long and people were so slow in getting their belongings that my excitement slowly turned to anxiety. What would the United States be like? Would its people like me? I clutched my small carry-on tightly to my chest, just as I had done when I nervously crossed into West Germany.

We stepped off the plane into a sea of chaos. There were people everywhere. I had to pay careful attention not to lose sight of my family as we maneuvered through the crowds. Finally, we made our way out of the airport and into the city.

I was in complete awe. I had never seen buildings so tall. The streets were even more crowded than the airport. Everyone seemed to be in a hurry to get somewhere. Some people were yelling for taxis, while others were trying to sell their goods to people passing by. There was so much commotion I didn't know where to look first. And while I was utterly amazed, I also felt vaguely frightened. After all, I'd never been in a city so large. What if I were to get lost? No one would ever be able to find me.

George called out for a taxi, but none would stop for him. He looked smart in his blue-gray military uniform. But that didn't impress any of the taxi drivers. Each one drove right past him, only to pull over for another person a little ways down the street. I could tell that George was getting frustrated, and my mother noticed too. She waved her hand out for a taxi, and finally one pulled over for us.

After a thrilling drive of a few miles, our driver pulled up outside a large hotel. The building was probably twenty or thirty stories high, much higher than any building I had ever been in before. And the furnishings were the nicest I had ever seen in my life. We were obviously rich. America truly was the land of opportunity I had heard so much about.

We rode up the elevator to our floor, and George led us to our room. Georgia, Barbara, and I immediately ran to the window and looked down to the ground. The people below us looked so tiny. I looked to my left and my right and could hardly count the number of cars below us. I wondered if everyone in the United States owned a car.

"Come on, kids. Let's take a bath," Mama said, motioning for the girls to follow her to the bathroom.

I continued to the stand in the window, wondering what my matka would have thought of all this. I knew she would have been as thrilled as I was. I only wished she were with me.

My thoughts were interrupted when George told us he was taking us all out for a nice dinner. And he wasn't lying. The restaurant we walked to from our hotel was more beautiful than any restaurant I had ever seen. The people were all dressed nicely, and the tables were set with wine glasses and candles.

The waiter brought us menus, but I couldn't read what was written on mine. George assured me he would order for me. He was in such a good mood since arriving in the United States. I could tell he had missed his homeland while being stationed in Germany, just as I was missing Poland. And aside from the minor frustration he had with the taxi drivers who wouldn't pull over for him, I think he was relieved to be back where people spoke his native language.

As we sipped water from our wine glasses, George smiled at me over his glass. I was slightly taken aback. George had never been unkind to me, but he had always been somewhat distant. He bought me clothes and food and tried to include me in every family outing, but he also seemed to wish I had never come. In America, though, it was different. Even though we still couldn't communicate well, he was laughing and joking with all of us. For the first time I felt like maybe we could be a family after all. Maybe he could be the father I had never had.

———————————————————

The time we had in New York was a whirl of fun. We walked up and down the streets of New York, looking in shop windows, stopping to eat in little cafés, and taking in the spectacular view of the immense city. My favorite outing was when we visited the Empire State Building.

Not too long before I had literally been a prisoner in my own city back in Poland. In a short time I had visited many countries and was now in one of the greatest countries in the world. I felt such a release as I stood on top of the Empire State Building looking down on the tiny people below. I was free!

It was one of the best moments of my life, but it came with a steep price. My matka wasn't with me. She was still a prisoner of Communism. She would never be able to leave Poland. And I might never see her again.

As we made our way down to the gift shop in the Empire State Building, I saw a couple of postcards for sale. One of them had a picture of the Statue of Liberty. The statue meant freedom to me, and I wanted to share a tiny bit of that freedom with Matka. I wanted her to know I had made it to the land of opportunity. She would be so proud.

After a few days touring New York, George informed us that we had to take a train south, because he had been stationed somewhere in Georgia. When we arrived at the train station, I was amazed at its complexity. The train station in Toruń was pretty simple. There were two tracks, one on either side of the platform, and one waiting deck. At this train station, there were hundreds of track lines going every which way.

The train station itself was like a museum. There were stores and restaurants, and around every corner a boy could be found shining shoes. I stood and watched one boy for a moment before George told me that I should get my cowboy boots shined. So I got my first shoe shine. I felt like royalty. George gave the boy some money, and he seemed really grateful. He kept saying, "Thank you, sir. Thank you!" That seemed to make George happy, so he told us we were all going to have breakfast together.

Finally, after breakfast and some people-watching, our train arrived. There was a gentleman there telling people where to go, so George showed him our tickets. The man pointed farther down the train, about three or four boxcars from the front. We were greeted by several black men who took our suitcases and helped us board the train.

After about 15 minutes, the train wheels started churning, and we made our way out of the city. I sat by the window, watching all the tall buildings slowly disappear. Later the conductor came in and pulled out little beds for me and the girls. As I lay down that night, wondering where we were headed, my thoughts returned again to the fact that we were moving even farther away from my matka. I began to feel scared. I didn't want to go through rejection again. I didn't want to deal with any more pain. So for the first time, I prayed.

"God, I think You know me, but I never really talked to You before. I'm scared. I don't know where I'm going or what is going to happen to me when I get there. Life seems to be going pretty well right now, but it never stays really good for long. Can You help me to adjust to my new life? Can You help me find happiness?"

The room was silent. All I could hear were the wheels of the train chugging along the track. Was God even listening? Did He even care?

"God, if You'll just take care of my mamusia, I'll be happy. Please, just take care of her."

If He didn't answer any other prayer, I wanted Him to at least answer that one request.

— — — — — — — — — — — — — — — —

When our train finally arrived in Georgia, we were happy to get out into the fresh air. It was the fall of 1959, and the weather felt really nice for that time of year. Back in Poland, the leaves would already be falling in the middle of September, but in Georgia it almost felt like summer.

As I looked around me, I realized that a group of black people had gathered together at one side of the platform, while all the white people who were on the train gathered on the other side. George motioned to us that we should follow him, but I felt strange. Mama and I were the only white people standing in the midst of black faces.

Already I could sense the hate and anger between the two groups of people. Why were these people being separated? Was it like when the German children at the orphanage were separated from the Polish kids? If so, I wanted to be on the side that wasn't going to get beaten and abused. I had already endured enough of that. Whatever it was, things weren't right. I could feel it.

George led the way to a waiting bus that was going to take us to the military base where he was stationed. As we loaded the bus, George immediately made his way to the back. As we got closer to the back, it became really hot. I motioned for my family to sit in the front where it was cooler and there were more seats.

As I made my way back up to the front, George jumped up and grabbed me by the arm, pulling me with him to the back of the bus. I didn't understand at first, but as more people got on the bus, I saw that once again whites and blacks were separated. I didn't understand this strange sort of hatred, but I would need to learn the rules to survive in this foreign culture.

These new rules on how to behave while in public were apparently well-established and accepted by everyone else. The black people on the bus seemed to know their place and didn't complain. I could sense the discontent brewing beneath the surface, however.

Unfortunately, I soon learned that the segregation of whites and blacks did not remain within the confines of public transportation. As soon as we arrived in the town outside the base, people treated us differently. In Germany, people had simply pointed or stared. Here in Georgia it was different. People would yell and spit on us. One man threw dirt at us as we walked past him.

Stores were even worse. People shouted at us as we entered, and a woman who otherwise looked respectable spit in my mother's face. They looked at each of us with hatred in their eyes. I just didn't understand. Why were we not welcome? I felt like I had done something wrong, but I knew I hadn't. What was wrong with these people?

Those first few days in Georgia were only the beginning of the overwhelming hatred people had toward me and my family. We rarely ate out, because every time we entered a restaurant we were forced to sit in the back by the bathrooms. I hated eating there. It smelled like ripe sewage all of the time.

When we did choose to eat out at restaurants, our choices were limited. Few opened their doors to both whites and blacks. Generally, restaurants owned by white men only served people with white skin. And while restaurants owned by black men and women were less hostile about serving a white person, there was a definite sense that we were not welcome. We were a mixed family. And nobody approved of the mixing of races.

As if I didn't have enough trouble with people not accepting me, Mama decided to enroll me in school. In town, there was a school for white children and a school for black children. I tried attending the white school first, but I was constantly being picked on for being a "nigger lover." I didn't even know what that meant, but I had a feeling it had something to do with the color of my sisters' skin.

When I wasn't being bullied or beaten up because of my family, it was because I couldn't speak English well. No one liked me. And to be perfectly honest, I didn't like anyone else. I thought America would be different from Poland and Germany, but I was wrong. No matter where a person is from, hatred can consume them. People seemed born to hate. So I hated everyone right back.

After a month or two, the principal of the school I was attending thought that I might have an easier time if I attended the black school. White students refused to accept me, so he assumed I might find a kinder audience at the all-black school. Not true. On the very first day I attended the black school, I was jumped from behind and beaten by a couple of angry guys.

No matter where I went, I wasn't accepted. Everywhere I turned, people despised me without knowing anything about me.

I had learned a lot about hatred as a child, but it was only when I saw how cruel people could be to my sisters that I began to understand the depths of hatred. One day my sisters and I were walking to a park when we happened to pass by a couple of rowdy, white teenagers. When they saw the three of us, they immediately started in on us.

"Hey, you! Hey, nigger lover!" they called out to me.

I didn't respond. Reacting to their stupidity only worsened the blows they gave.

"Look at me when I'm talking to you, boy!"

I stared straight ahead, pushing my sisters to walk a little faster. As I did, Barbara dropped the toy she had been holding, which gave the teenagers the opportunity to approach us.

"God didn't intend for whites and negroes to have children. You're a spawn of the devil!" the lankiest of the teenagers cackled as he pointed at Barbara. Then, before I could react, he spit directly in her face, causing her to cry out in shock.

I had done my best to stay in control of my anger, but something inside of me erupted. I had been suppressing everything for so long that I couldn't hold back any longer. I became that little boy in the orphanage again, defending the honor of those who couldn't defend themselves.

I charged at the boy with all my might, knocking him to the ground. He never saw me coming. I picked myself off the ground before he could get up and began swinging my fists left and right. He screamed obscenities, but that only fueled my anger. He got in a few punches himself, but he looked much worse than me. His nose was all bloody, and his lip was split open.

I was so intent on teaching him a lesson for spitting on my sister that I didn't notice the policemen arrive. Apparently the other boys with him had called in the police.

As they dragged me off the kid, I noticed for the first time that Barbara and Georgia were cowering together near the bushes, crying. They had witnessed the entire event. I hadn't thought about that when I was hitting their assailant. I tried to tell the policeman that this kid had started the fight by spitting on my sister, but he would hear none of it. He told me that I was a liar and that I was lucky he wasn't going to haul me off to jail. I learned then that, just like in Poland, the police were not to be trusted.

———————————————————

We didn't stay in Georgia very long after that. George was re-assigned to a base in Oklahoma, so we made our way west. I had little hope that the people would treat us any better than they had in Georgia. And for the most part I was right.

The hatred in Oklahoma wasn't as transparent as it had been in Georgia. People still stared and felt the need to call out obscenities when we passed as a family, but for the most part there was little fear of people physically attacking us. I wasn't nearly as afraid to walk the streets with my sisters as I had been in Georgia.

I did feel less inclined to be at home, however. After moving to Oklahoma, George began drinking more. He complained a lot about not getting the respect he deserved. People treated him like a nobody, which made him angry. After all, he had defended the Unites States while stationed abroad, and now people treated him like all that he had done and worked for meant nothing. The social tensions of the United States began to take a toll on our household.

At first, his heavy drinking led him to say nasty things to my mother or to me about being privileged because we were born white.

"If anyone knew anything about what losers the two of you are, they wouldn't look down on me more than they do you!" he would yell.

Mama rarely responded to his tirades. Instead, she would try to comfort him, telling him that he deserved the respect he had earned while being stationed in Germany. I, too, never responded. Instead, I quietly began to despise him.

Soon, his tirades turned physical. The abuse usually started with my mother and then moved on to me and my sisters. He was especially brutal to my sister, Georgia.

"You aren't my child. You're too white! What? You think you're better than me?" he would scream at her.

She was only a small child. She never knew what she did to deserve the beatings. Yet she was always seeking his approval. She would do anything for him. Up until he started drinking, he had been a good father to his children. The alcohol made him want nothing to do with them, unless he was yelling at them or beating them.

When we were re-assigned to Fort Riley, Kansas, the abuse took a turn for the worse. George came home one night after spending several hours at the local bar. He had grown agitated from the way he had been treated earlier in the day, and the agitation festered into rage. When he walked in the house, we knew it would be a long, painful night.

First he started in on Mama, telling her that she was ungrateful and no good, but soon his attention turned to my sisters. I don't remember the exact thing that set him off, but he took his belt and began beating those two little girls like never before. His swings were rough and came down hard on their skin. They screamed in terror, but he held them both down and kept beating them over and over again.

My rage set in. No one should harm a child. No one. I knew that George was strong, nearly twice the size of me. I was just a weak, 17-year-old kid. But I couldn't stand there and watch him brutally abuse my sisters. I knew what beatings felt like. I never wanted to see my sisters suffer the same.

"Stop hurting them, now!" I yelled out to him in English, my accent still thick on the little bit of the language I had picked up.

George stopped mid-swing, my sisters still screaming, and turned to me.

"What did you say, loser?"

"They're babies. Leave them alone." My voice trembled, not because I was scared, but because I could feel the adrenaline of rage pulsing through my veins.

"I'll show you who is a baby!" he said, jumping off my sisters and rushing me.

I hardly had time to react before he knocked me to the ground. He pinned me, and I could barely breathe as he put his knee in my chest. He punched me in the face a few times before jumping off me again.

For a moment, I thought it was all over. But before I could sit up, he was back. Only this time he carried a thick steel chain. He swung the chain around him, smashing it into my back. He did it over and over again, gaining momentum and force. He wasn't going to stop, I could tell. He wanted to kill me.

I could hear my mother and my sisters screaming at him to stop, but he didn't pay any attention to them. He was intent on his prey. Luckily for me, the booze began to have an effect on him. Eventually he grew tired, putting down the chain a moment to recuperate.

I didn't hesitate. I ran into my room, locking the door behind me. I knew I had to get out of there. I grabbed a few documents, a picture of my matka, and a picture of my sisters. I could hear George screaming at the girls and making his way down the hall to my room. Frantic, I climbed out my open window and began running down the street.

As I ran down our street, I could hear George yelling at Barbara, who must have seen me running as she looked out the window. She ran behind me, crying for me not to leave. She wanted me to stay with her, but I had taken enough. There was no reason for me to stay. My life was miserable. It had been better when I was in Poland. At least there I knew what was going on half the time. And while I had grown to love my sisters and my birth mother, they weren't enough reason for me to endure abuse from a man I didn't love or even care for.

In all the time I spent with my mother, I still hadn't learned anything new about my past. I still didn't know why she had left me to die alone as a child. And I couldn't comprehend why she would stay with a man who treated her children as horribly as George did. Clearly she didn't love us as much as she said she did. If she did, she would never have abandoned me in the first place, and she certainly wouldn't tolerate George's abuse. My matka would never let a man abuse her like that. And if she ever saw him beat me, she would have done even worse to him. She was a true mother. She sacrificed everything for me, and I wasn't even really her son.

I hated leaving my sisters, but I could only think of saving myself. Blood ran down my face and back, but I didn't stop. And I never once looked back. I just kept running and running and running. I ran until I couldn't physically run anymore. I moved off the road and lay down, exhausted.

———————————————

When I awoke the next morning, I realized I had slept in a cemetery. A little lump of grass near a graveside served as my pillow. I wasn't scared, though. I knew I had to keep moving. I didn't know where I was going; I just knew the sun was in the east. That was the direction I was going to walk. I would walk all the way back to Poland if I had to.

After I had been walking for miles, a farmer driving a pickup truck pulled over and asked if I needed a ride. I accepted, glad to be off my feet, and we rode 20 or 30 miles into the next town where he was stopping to buy some supplies. Before dropping me off, he kindly gave me five dollars to buy some food.

I immediately ran to the nearest store and got as much food as my five dollars would buy me. I swallowed each bite quickly, not having eaten in over a day. My thoughts turned back to my sisters. Were they okay? Would they be okay without me there? For a moment, I considered turning back for their sakes, but my feet just wouldn't take the steps. The previous evening was already in my past; I had to move on. There was no turning back. I was walking toward my future now. I needed a future away from all the pain. I needed to experience true freedom.

So I kept walking east. I received a couple of rides here and there, but for the most part I walked alone with my thoughts. Finally, around Higginsville, Missouri, 180 miles from where I had started, a sheriff's car pulled alongside of me.

"Where are you headed to, boy?" asked the sheriff as he rolled down his window.

I shrugged, unable to respond in his language.

"Running away, are you?" he asked.

I nodded.

"Hop in the car, son." He got out of the car and opened the back door for me.

Exhausted, filthy, and hungry, I didn't care where he would take me. I didn't even care if he was arresting me. I just needed to eat something and lay down. If anything, I was glad to be getting off my feet.

I slid into the backseat and noticed that I wasn't the only one in the vehicle with the sheriff. Another man was sitting in the passenger seat. There was something different about him, but I couldn't put my finger on it.

"Where are you from, son?" asked the man.

I understood his question. This was one I had heard often.

"Poland."

I had been telling people I was from Germany, because that's what my mother always said. But Germany wasn't my home. My home was in Poland.

"Well, that's pretty far away, I'd say," the man chuckled to himself. "And where did you run from?"

"Kansas," I said. I didn't want to tell him too much more. I didn't know if I could really trust these two men. I began to get a little worried that they might take me back to the military base with George and my family.

"Well, we'll get this all straightened out. In the meantime, my name is Ike Skelton. What's yours?" he asked, putting out his hand for a handshake.

"Peter," I said, grabbing his hand. Our shake felt slightly awkward, because he offered me his left hand. It was then that I noticed that his other hand was all shriveled. He saw me looking at his disabled hand and smiled.

"No one has a perfect life, kid. Not even the best of us." And he turned back around in his seat.

We rode another couple of miles before arriving at the local police station in Lexington, Missouri. Once there I was questioned a bit. The interview was nothing like the Soviet questioning I had endured in Poland. Instead of a bombardment of questions right off the bat, they offered me some food and drink and calmly asked what had happened.

I did my best to explain the situation to them in broken English. I'm afraid much of what I had to say was lost on them, though. I did manage to give them my full name and that I had run away from Fort Riley, which seemed to please them.

Ike Skelton was there during all of the questioning. Although he wasn't an officer of the law, he seemed quite interested in my story. I later learned that he was a local attorney, who worked closely with the police on various cases.

Skelton turned to Eugene Darnell, the sheriff, and said in a lowered voice, "If you need a place for him to stay, he can stay with me for a night or two until we can figure out the rest of his story. It's pretty obvious he's running from an abusive home. Did you see his back?"

The sheriff eyed me from where he sat.

"We'll definitely have to look into the matter," he said.

"In the meantime, I'll try to get a more permanent home for him to stay in and see if I can't find some sort of translator for him," said Skelton.

Sheriff Darnell nodded in agreement, and I went home with Ike Skelton that evening.

———————————————

Over the next couple of days, Ike Skelton drove me around town, buying me clothes and getting me acquainted with the area.

In between our drives, we spent time talking at the police station. I gave him and the sheriff some of the papers I had taken with me before running away, which gave them more of an idea of where I was coming from and why I was in the United States in the first place.

At one point they brought in a translator, but the man spoke German, not Polish. He immediately told the two men that I wasn't a German native.

"I don't understand, though. He's got a German passport," Sheriff Darnell said.

"He might have a German passport, but he is not German, sir. He hardly speaks the language at all. He claims to be Polish. Get him a Polish translator, instead," the translator responded, walking out the door after demanding his payment.

Ike Skelton sat down beside me.

"Why do you have a German passport if you aren't German?" he asked me.

I tried to explain, but it seemed like no one could quite understand how I managed to grow up in Poland, yet be a German citizen. I, myself, had trouble understanding the entire situation. My poor command of the English language didn't help matters.

Years later I would tell people I was from Greenland when they asked where I was from after hearing my accent. Most people didn't even know where Greenland was located, so it helped me avoid answering unwanted questions. At this point, though, I wasn't that clever.

After a couple of days of trying to find answers to their unanswerable questions, Ike Skelton and Sheriff Darnell resolved that they would never quite get the whole story. In the meantime, they found a family who said they would let me live with them. The Homfelds needed an extra hand to work the small farm they owned, so they took me in quite happily and taught me my chores right away.

Ike Skelton checked in on me every once in awhile to see that I was all right. He also helped me enroll in the military school outside of Lexington, so I could get some education. After a few months, I went to live with the Thoman family on their farm in Higginsville.

They had three teenage sons, so I got to enjoy living the life of a teenager. When the boys and I weren't in school, we were working on the farm or racing their Delta 88 and Buick on dirt roads. I met my first American girlfriend, Mary Linda Rekhopf, who introduced me to teenage dances, the James Dean fashion, and malted milk-shakes. For a time, I was at peace.

But I never lost my desire to return to Poland. I wrote my matka often, telling her where I ended up and how I was managing. Whenever I got any money I would save a little up and go to town to buy her something to send in a package. I knew she could sell or trade what I gave her for good food. I just wished I could somehow package myself up and send it her way. Then we'd both be happy.

I never wrote my birth mother. The more time I spent with the Thoman family on the farm, the more I realized how angry I still was with my mother. They were a loving family that honestly cared for the well-being of their children. I could never imagine Mrs. Thoman abandoning her boys.

My mother, on the other hand, had abandoned me as a baby and then taken me from the one woman who had ever truly loved me, only to subject me to beatings from the man I was supposed to look up to as a father figure. I understood that she wasn't the one who was abusive, but she allowed it to happen. If it hadn't been for her, I would never have met George. She put me in that situation, just as she had put me in every orphanage by abandoning me as a baby. She didn't love me; she never loved me. I would never go back. From that point on, my birth mother was dead to me.

Chapter 15

I was never fully able to run from my past. Over forty years after I ran away from home and declared my mother dead, my past caught up with me on that hot summer day in Florida. I was again pondering the questions that my mother had left unanswered all those years ago. And I still needed answers.

Some of the answers I was finding were more confusing than comforting. I endured a lot in my childhood, but nothing prepared me for the news that everything I had thought to be true about my life was a lie. I grew up believing that my mother was a full-blooded German. I had assumed she was somehow aligned with the Nazi Party. After all, most German citizens were. I was even under the impression that my father was a Nazi soldier. But none of that was true. The truth I now had to deal with was so much more difficult to accept. *My life began in a concentration camp.* It was like some kind of sick joke.

After that first phone call from the Red Cross, I began to learn more about my family history. My mother had indeed been Jewish. She was arrested and placed in Stutthof Concentration Camp with her sister (the aunt I had met back in Germany so many years ago). My grandmother had also been arrested. When she resisted, the Nazi soldiers executed her on the spot, right in front of my mother and aunt.

To make matters worse, it turned out my grandfather, a fervent member of the Nazi Party, did nothing to stop the arrests. Guilty of marrying a Jewish woman, he allowed his family to be taken away to be slaughtered. He was a selfish man, wanting to marry a woman nearly the same age as his daughters. He saw their arrests as an opportunity to rid himself of his "problematic" family. He managed to save my uncle from such a fate, however — perhaps a partial explanation of why my uncle felt so uncomfortable in my mother's presence. My grandfather had him sent to the front in France, instead. How he hid his son's Jewish heritage is still unknown.

Several years after that first phone call, my head would still spin whenever I tried to process all the pieces of my past that had come to light. My own grandfather had turned against his family, allowing his pregnant daughter to be taken to a concentration camp, where I was later born. And while that story was outrageous on its own, I still couldn't get past the fact that I was actually Jewish.

I needed more answers. I needed to understand. I needed to find myself, so I could make sense of the chaos of my life.

One afternoon after swimming through all the information yet again, I heaved myself into a chair at my kitchen table and dropped my head. The house was silent; all I could hear was my pounding headache. My wife and kids had left an hour earlier to go grocery shopping. I felt so alone. No one could understand what I was going through. My wife tried, but she just didn't get why this was destroying everything I knew to be true about myself. Sure, we had a huge family of eight kids. I was pretty good at surrounding myself with people, yet no one could answer my questions. No one could help me.

Although most of my questions arose from the information I had received in the last couple of years, it wasn't the first time I had tried to piece together the truth about my past. In the mid-1970s I managed to get back into Poland after a series of interrogations by the border control. Once there, I found my matka.

She immediately embraced me as though I were the child I was when we parted. She wanted to know all about the adventures I experienced in the United States. So we talked into the late hours of the night, just as we had done when I was a boy. I felt so relieved to see her. She was doing well, still cleaning houses and making a living performing several other odd jobs. I tried asking her some questions about my past, but she was still as vague as she had always been. Though I prodded her for answers, I never did learn how I ended up in her care. Every time I pushed her for an answer, she would respond that it was in the past and to forget it.

I also tried to find out who my father was. But every lead I had turned into a dead end. It seemed that no one wanted to talk about the events during the war. Everyone was so secretive that I eventually gave up searching. I couldn't help but wonder whether there were some pieces of my life that would never be known.

All was not lost, however. By traveling back to Poland, I was able to get in touch with both Henryk and Dieter, whose futures looked bright. Henryk had fallen in love with a spunky woman, who always had him on some new adventure. And Dieter had married Ursula, just as I had hoped. They even had children, two of them named Piotr. He called the first Piotr One and the second Piotr Two. I felt so honored.

I probably would have stayed in Poland indefinitely had my matka not made me promise to return to the United States to ensure a better life for myself. I knew that, once again, my matka was right. I had to leave. There was no way I could support her within the confines of Communist Poland. If I returned to the United States, however, I could continue sending her money and care packages.

And for the most part, I had done well for myself in America. But, just when I thought I had "made it," I fumbled it all away and hit rock bottom. My first marriage ended in shambles. I remarried, but that didn't last either, ending as quickly as it had begun. I had four children, but I was alone.

When I met my wife, Val, things slowly began to change. We had a whirlwind romance, marrying after only six short weeks. We hadn't been married long when Val mentioned her desire to attend church, as she wanted her children to have the same opportunity to learn about God as she had as a child. So, although neither of us was very devout, we found ourselves returning to one particular church week after week. There was something about the people there that drew us in — they were genuine. Since it was a fairly large congregation, we were able to sit back and observe things before becoming involved in the various ministries the church had to offer. We began attending a Bible study, which provided us with the opportunity to ask questions and dialogue with others about God's Word.

As we learned more about God and became more involved with the church, I began to understand what my matka had told me about God so many years ago. For the first time, God began to be real to me. He wasn't an impersonal and cruel deity watching me from afar. He became very present in my life. The more we read and learned from the Bible, the more my life seemed to fall into place. God was at the center of our lives. And for once, I wasn't alone in my journey. Val was right beside me.

But the turning point in my relationship with God occurred one day when I was alone. I had decided to attend our church's men's event called The Emmaus Retreat. It was a powerful weekend of ministry and contemplation. During a moment of quiet and solitude, I began praying outside in a rose garden. It was there that I saw the face of Jesus before me. When I looked into His eyes, He took me on a journey to my childhood. Through each new image and reminder of my past, the Lord assured me that He loved me and that He had been with me all of my life. I wept and promised to follow Him and be true to Him all the days of my life.

After this, I was a changed man. I fully accepted the fact that God was in control of my life. I had finally learned that when I was in control, things never turned out right. Of course, there were times here and there when I would try to take that control back, but I knew deep down that if I wanted or needed answers, the only one who could provide them was God.

"God," I cried out, "please help me. I don't know what to do or where to turn. All this information is too much for me. And yet, it isn't enough. I don't know anything about my past really. I don't know who I am or why I'm even here."

I lifted my head from the table and looked upward.

"I just feel like I should have died a long time ago. I should have died with those people in the concentration camp. I should have died with Star that night! I shouldn't be here...why am I still here?"

The house was silent, but in the stillness I suddenly had an answer.

Go back to the beginning.

I stood up from the table, my headache dissipating. Yes! I had to go back to the beginning. I had to return to the place I was born. I knew I would find the peace I was looking for within the gates of my initial imprisonment.

Yet even as the excitement about returning to Poland rose up within me, reality set in — there was no way we could afford an overseas trip.

Here was another chance to choose either control or surrender. I chose surrender. If God really wanted me to go back to Poland, He would make a way. And He did just that. A few weeks later, someone blessed us with five roundtrip tickets to Poland. Not only would Val be able to come with me, but three of my kids — Sandy, my stepdaughter who was on summer vacation from college; and our two youngest, Juliana and Phillip, who were young teenagers. Not only had God provided a means for me to go back, but I wouldn't have to go alone.

— — — — — — — — — — — — — — —

"Come on, come on! We've got to get going, or we're going to miss the plane!" I called out to my family. They were always lagging behind.

"We're going to make it just fine. Don't worry so much. We've got two and a half hours before our flight departs. All we have to do is check the bags and go through security," my wife said, trying to calm my nerves.

"Well, we don't know how long the lines will be!"

She and the kids rolled their eyes at me, but they picked up the pace. I could hear my three kids laughing about something behind me, but I kept speed walking to the baggage check. I wasn't going to be slowed down. I had to make this flight. I had to see Stutthof Concentration Camp with my own eyes. This wasn't fun and games; this was my life. I had to find out who I was.

— — — — — — — — — — — — — — —

We arrived in Frankfurt the next day, hopped in our rental car and began driving. The kids fell asleep in the back, exhausted from the long trip and the jet lag. I didn't let the jet lag phase me. My adrenaline was pumping. I wanted to show my family everything. I wanted to show them Berlin, Vienna, Salzburg, and my hometown of Toruń. We planned on driving through as many countries as our two weeks allowed. But we'd also be visiting Stutthof. Part of me longed to be there immediately; the other part of me wished to avoid it altogether.

After driving through Germany for the first few days of our trip, we finally approached the border between Poland and Germany. I could feel my legs beginning to go limp. I remembered previous border crossings. I remembered the questioning and interrogations. I remembered being told that I would be killed if I ever tried re-entering the country. Of course, that had been decades ago, and the Soviets had lost control of Poland in 1989. It was 2002, and Communism was no longer a way of life in the country where I grew up. Even so, I could feel my nerves getting the best of me.

"What's wrong, Dad?" my son Phil asked from the backseat.

"Quiet! We're almost at the border!" I ordered, my heart quickening.

"Why do we have to be quiet at the border?" my wife asked.

"It doesn't matter," I snapped. "Do you have your passports? Sandy, give me your passport."

"Hold on a second. I have to find it," she said calmly from her seat in the back.

I began to feel frantic. What did she mean she had to find it? How could she have misplaced it? We were going to be stopped and interrogated. I just knew it. I could feel my stomach doing flips.

"Oh, here it is," she said nonchalantly, handing me her passport.

I almost felt relieved, but we were already at the border. I could see the police officers and Polish military in their booths as we approached the checkpoint.

"*Dzien dobre.* Passport?" the guard said, holding out his hand.

I fumbled for all five of our passports and nearly dropped them as I handed them out the window.

"Americans?" the man asked.

"Yes, yes," I said, wondering what his next question would be.

"Good," he said, stamping each passport. "Welcome to Poland. Have a nice visit."

I was amazed at his perfect English. I was even more amazed at the lack of questioning.

"See, that wasn't hard at all," Val said.

I ignored her comment. She didn't understand. She wasn't with me the first time I crossed that border. If she had been, she would know why my legs went weak every time we crossed into another country.

After driving another 430 kilometers, we entered the town of Sztutowo, Poland. I knew the concentration camp had to be somewhere within the town limits. We drove around, looking for any sign of the place, but we couldn't find anything. I noticed a little drugstore in the distance, so I pulled up and ran inside to ask for directions.

My Polish had grown rusty, but I did my best to make my request clear. The young woman seemed to understand after the second try. She told me that if I continued driving up the road we were on for a kilometer or two, we couldn't miss it. I knew it was nearby, but it hadn't really hit me how close we were to my birthplace. My feet turned to lead as I made my way back to the vehicle.

"Are we close?" Val asked.

"Yes, it's just up the road."

My family must have sensed the dread I was feeling, because as we got back on the road, no one spoke a word.

"Keep your eye out for a sign," I mumbled to them, my voice barely audible.

My wife and kids stared out the window, looking for some indication of the camp. We drove along for a bit, still seeing nothing. The woman at the drugstore must have been mistaken. We had already driven a few kilometers, and still we weren't seeing the camp.

Then I felt it. I could hear voices calling out to me.

I slammed on the brakes.

"What's wrong?" Val nearly screamed. She looked wildly about, trying to see if we had hit an animal or something.

"We're here," I told her, the tears welling up in my eyes.

"What do you mean?" Sandy asked. "There's nothing here."

As we looked around, all we could see were tall, lush trees and a set of train tracks that looked old and rusty.

"Dad, are you okay?" Phillip asked, concerned.

They were right. There was nothing on the road that indicated Stutthof was nearby, but I knew it. I could sense it. The hair on my arms was standing on end.

I took my foot off the brake and coasted a few meters.

"Dad was right! Look, Mom!" Juli cried out, pointing just beyond a set of trees.

On the side of the road, hidden behind some branches, was a large sign bearing the name: STUTTHOF.

I lost it.

I could hardly see through all my tears. I was a mess, but somehow I managed to pull in the drive and park in the little parking lot.

"This is it. I recognize it from the pictures," I said through my tears.

I sobbed even more. This was where it all began. Where my life took a turn for the worse, right at the very beginning.

We sat in the car for a few moments before getting out. Val shoved a few tissues in my direction, and I cleaned off my face. I couldn't sit any longer. I had to face my past.

The place was peaceful. The camp almost looked inviting, with its lawn freshly cut and the birds chirping in the trees. I could feel the evil simmering underneath it all, though. The evils of the past couldn't be masked by the calming façade of the present.

I marched through the gates, barely stopping to glance at the surroundings. My tears turned to anger. I could feel all the hatred I had ever experienced in my life begin to simmer below the surface. I couldn't let it out, though. Not here. Not now. I had to be strong for my family.

To my right was the commandants' headquarters. The building was large and beautiful, with big open windows and tall pillars. It looked like a summer villa for getting away from the world. The building's past, however, was not pretty. While doing research on the camp, I had come across a picture of Hitler's right-hand man,

Himmler, standing in front of this very building. Nazi flags hung from the pillars behind him. The picture made me sick to my stomach.

So I turned to my left, instead. Before me was a small, rickety wooden barrack. I walked in and saw the pile of thousands of shoes that had been stolen from the prisoners who lived and died in the camp. As I stared into the midst of the gray mass, one pair caught my eye. It was clearly a pair of baby's shoes. I choked on my tears, nearly gagging.

If the men responsible for the deaths of these innocent people were still alive, I knew I could kill them myself. They deserved to die for the horrific pain and anger I was feeling.

My family stood behind me as I continued to stare into the pile of shoes. I didn't even bother trying to hold back the tears. There was just too much emotion for me to handle. Juliana came up behind me and gave me a hug. I could feel her love, and I held her tightly. Why should my children have to see this? Why should they have to see the obvious pain I was going through because of the atrocities of these few inhumane individuals? This wasn't anything a child should see. Yet, here we were.

We walked along the grounds some more, noticing the bombed-out barracks alongside those that were still standing. Inside each remaining barrack was information regarding the history of the camp and the various medical procedures that were carried out within its gates.

As we entered one of the barracks, I noticed a little table with various metal tools lying on it. I read the blurb of information about the contents of the room and found that it was where abortions were carried out. Almost every child born at Stutthof was murdered. Those who were allowed to survive were taken for experimental treatments to the hospital in Tiegenhof (present day Nowy Dwor Gdansk, Poland). I must have been one of those children.

I rushed through the rest of the barracks, barely reading any of the material. My adrenaline was pumping, and I had to move. I had to do something with the anger.

As we made our way out of the barracks and into the far end of the field, we found ourselves in front of a gas chamber. To the right of the gas chamber was another larger building that housed several ovens, which were used to burn the dead bodies of the camp's prisoners. My blood went cold. Somehow I had managed to avoid these as a baby. But why? Why was I saved and not others? Why me?

I had to get out of there. I was wrong for coming in the first place. What had I been thinking? Why did I think I would gain any answers by coming to such a wretched place?

"We've got to go!" I called to my family as they were still taking in the scene before them.

They hurried toward me.

"What's the matter?" Val asked.

"I can't be here anymore."

"But, don't you want to try to get any records?"

"What's the point?" I yelled.

"We drove all this way. I thought that's what you wanted."

"I can't be here, Val! This place is evil. I can't be in this place!" I yelled, storming ahead of the rest of them.

I knew she was right, though. If there was any chance that the camp did have documents for me, I had to at least try.

I walked up to the records office, which was once the commandants' headquarters. I tried opening the door, but it was locked. I pounded on the door, hoping someone might be inside to answer. Val and the kids caught up to me and tried a few other doors.

"Wait, what does this sign say?" Val asked me. She couldn't read Polish.

I skimmed the sign.

"The office is closed on Mondays. It will be open again tomorrow. Forget it. I knew this was a waste of time. I wish I never came here."

I swiftly turned around and marched down the steps and out the gate. I didn't look back. I wanted out of that place. If I never saw it again, I would be a happy man.

Chapter 16

We drove for an hour before I finally stopped at a little hostel on the side of the road. The entire car ride had been in silence. No one said a word. Every once in awhile Val would pat my shoulder and try to comfort me, but my anger still raged.

I hated what it all meant for my life. I hated that the main reason I had suffered so much as a child had been because of the hatred of some clearly demented men. Had I not been born in this concentration camp and been separated from my mother, I would never have ended up in those orphanages where I was raped and abused. I would have been normal. Instead, bottled up inside me was more anger and pain than any man should endure. And I blamed it all on the Nazis. They were the ones responsible for the direction my life had taken.

We stepped out of the car and stretched our legs. The hostel was built like a big log cabin and sat near a little lake, and we could see ducks wading in the water. For a moment, I stood mesmerized by a momma duck and her three little ducklings following closely behind her. If only I could have had that as a child.

"Can we eat?" Phillip asked, breaking me away from my thoughts.

We had gone without lunch. And while the last thing any of us really wanted to do was eat after what we had just witnessed, we were famished.

"Yes, son. They have a little restaurant inside. Let's go up to our rooms, put our stuff down, and then we'll eat."

After checking in, the kids went off to their room, and I walked into ours and put our bags down. Val immediately walked to the window and gazed out onto the lake below.

"Poland is really beautiful. I'm so glad we're here," she said, still facing the window.

I didn't respond. So far, our journey into Poland had been nothing but traumatizing for us all, and I knew it. I sat down on the edge of our bed and unzipped our suitcase.

Val turned toward me. I could tell from the look on her face that she wanted to tell me something.

"What?" I asked.

"I don't know. I just feel like I should say something, but I don't know if I should."

"Just say it." I knew she would anyway, so I figured she might as well get to the point.

"Well, after dinner I really think we should talk about what happened today," she said as she sat beside me on the bed.

"Why? There's nothing to talk about."

"Are you kidding? Of course there is! We know how hard it was for you today. We saw it on your face. Pete, you've got to talk about what you're feeling."

"I don't want to. It's just too hard!" I got up from the bed and walked toward the window.

"Fine. You don't have to tell me how you are feeling, but I definitely think we need to consider going back there tomorrow."

"What?" I spun around from where I was standing by the window. "Are you crazy, woman? I'm not going back there. You couldn't pay me to ever go back to that place."

"Pete, let's think about this logically. If we go back, we can try to find any documents they might have on you or your mother, because the records office will be open. Don't you want to get the proof in your hands?"

She had me there. I did want to get proof. Sure, I had documentation from the Red Cross, but I needed to see it in black and white from the concentration camp.

"I don't know if I can go back there," I told her, my resolve breaking a little.

"We're going to be there with you every step of the way, Pete. You're not alone in this." She smiled at me, stood up from the bed, and gave me a quick hug. "Come on, let's eat. We'll talk about this after dinner. I just want you to think about it. You don't have to make a decision right now."

She grabbed my hand, and we walked into the hall. The kids were just coming out of their room. Val was right. I wasn't alone here. My family was with me.

— — — — — — — — — — — — — — —

The next morning we drove back to Stutthof. This time, we knew exactly where it was located and exactly what to expect. None of us were very excited to be returning, but after talking more with Val the night before, I realized that it was the whole point of our trip to Europe. I was going to learn something. I could sense it.

I parked the car and once again made my way toward the dreaded gates of the camp. I was able to control my tears a bit more, but the lump in my throat was gigantic.

"I think I need to look around once more before going to the records office," I told my family, who nodded in understanding.

I knew that there was so much more to the camp than I had seen the previous day. I had been in such a hurry to get out that I missed a lot of the information available.

I walked past the barrack of shoes and into the main part of the camp. Again I saw before me the long lines of barracks that had been destroyed by the Soviets after the war. They were nothing but rubble. I stooped down and grabbed a piece of the rubble and put it in my pocket. It was a little piece of my history.

As I stood there looking around, I noticed that to the right of me were barracks I hadn't entered the previous day. I walked in that direction, dreading what I might learn.

The first barrack was full of panoramas and maps of what the camp looked like when the Nazis were in control. Stated in detail were the strategies behind the Nazis' desire to destroy the world's

Jewish population. As I walked from one barrack to the next, the information became more specific, detailing what went on at Stutthof. I learned that Stutthof was one of the largest soap-making factories of all the camps. The soap was not of ordinary design — it was made from the body fat of those who perished within the walls of the camp.

My anger from the previous day resurfaced as I continued reading. I wanted to see the people face-to-face who could run such a facility. I wanted to give them exactly what they deserved. How could anyone despise human life so much that they could actually manufacture and use soap made out of human bodies?

I left the stuffiness of the barracks, though I knew there was still more to see, and stepped out into the fresh air. I wasn't sure if we had made the right decision to come back.

"Hey, Pete! You should really see these," Sandy called from outside the last section of the barracks I had chosen to skip.

I hesitantly followed her to the door, Phillip alongside me.

"Are you two coming?" I asked Val and Juli from the doorway.

"I don't want to," Juliana protested.

"Why not?" I asked, not understanding.

"I just don't want to go in there, again," she insisted.

"I'll stay with her," Val chimed in.

I took a deep breath and stepped inside the dark building. Before me was a maze of dioramas and poster boards. As I walked among them, they began to lead me farther into the darkness that was my past. There were pictures of starved children and scarred women. There were pictures of the camp being liberated. There were pictures everywhere.

Suddenly I stopped short. On the poster board in front of me was the face of Max Pauly, the head commandant of Stutthof.

Sandy and Phil seemed to fade into the background as I stood face-to-face with the man who had destroyed my life. I stared into his vacant eyes, hoping to find some reason for his choosing to hurt so many. I received no answer.

I wanted to hurt him. I wanted to tear down that picture and rip it to shreds. He was the reason I suffered. This man was responsible for everything I had endured.

As I looked around, I noticed that to the right of him were pictures of his subordinate commandants. Looking at each one, I cursed their names and wished them to the worst confines of hell imaginable. I wanted them to be suffering for every ounce of pain I — or any of their victims — felt while living and dying at the camp.

All the hatred I had ever felt in my life would never equal the amount of hatred I felt standing before those pictures.

And then I heard a voice.

"Piotrusiu, Piotrusiu, Piotrusiu."

For a moment I wasn't sure what I heard. Was that my own voice in my head?

And then again, from nowhere, I heard the voice.

"Forgive them. Get down on your knees and forgive them."

No, I knew that voice clearly. I knew I would never think to actually forgive the men I held responsible for the destruction of my childhood. Only God would be so bold as to ask me to forgive these evil men.

"I can't! Why should I? They don't deserve my forgiveness," I screamed on the inside. There was no way I would ever forgive these men. I hated them too much.

Then, in words much bolder and clearer, I heard God say:

"Forgive them or I cannot forgive you."

I was stunned. What could that possibly mean? How could I be lumped into the same category as these men?

"Forgive me?" I asked. "But what did I do? I'm the victim. I was the one who suffered. Why would I need forgiveness?"

"You broke one of My commandments, Peter. 'Thou shalt honor thy mother and father.' Did you honor your mother?"

I never expected that answer. I never in a million years would have realized the depth of my sin toward my mother, but in that moment it came crashing over me.

I broke down in tears. He was right. I hadn't honored my mother. I had hated and despised her for abandoning me as a child. I didn't understand then the pain she must have endured for my sake. I was probably alive because of her sacrifices. Even though I didn't under-stand her first cries of *"mein leiber Peter"* that day in Germany, she had never stopped trying to communicate that message in a way that I could understand — "I love you, Peter. I love you, Peter." She *loved* me. And yet, I had turned my back on her. I had never given her the chance she deserved. I knew in that moment that I had to forgive my mother for the abandonment I had felt all of those years. But, more importantly, I had to ask for forgiveness from God.

I never felt so utterly convicted in my entire life. I didn't deserve forgiveness, just as these men didn't deserve forgiveness. Yet, God was offering it to me.

"Lord, You are right. Please forgive me for not loving my mother the way I should have loved her. Please, please forgive me for all the times I cursed her name and wished she were dead. Forgive me for not understanding until this very moment my own sin. I've been placing blame left and right, but my hatred is no different from these men."

Then, broken before the Lord, I fell to my knees before the pictures of Max Pauly and Paul Werner Hoppe, one of the other commandants of Stutthof.

I could barely get the words out, but they finally came.

"I forgive you."

A wave of emotion swept over me like nothing I've ever felt in my life, but I kept going. I knelt before the next picture and said the same.

"I forgive you."

Each time I knelt before another picture of a commandant and said those words, I felt more weight lift off me. The words came out easier with each picture I knelt before.

I'm not sure how many men and women I forgave that day. But when I finally stood up, all of the anger, hatred, and tension I had been carrying my entire life seemed to have melted away. I could breathe. I was able to stand before those men and know that they could no longer affect me. The hatred I had felt toward them would no longer have a hold on me. For the first time in my life, I was truly free.

I lifted up my arms before God and thanked Him for His gift of freedom. The answers I had been searching for didn't come from any document. My identity was in God. Sure, I still had questions about my past, but finding the answers to those questions wasn't going to help me discover who I was. I was completely clear on that now. I was God's child, and no one could ever convince me otherwise.

I was so full of gratitude and complete happiness that I began humming a praise song to God. I was aware of no one around me. It was just me and my Father. And He deserved all the praise that was in me.

When I finally turned around to leave the building and find my family, I saw Sandy and Phil standing against the wall watching me. I smiled at them, and they hesitantly smiled back. Sandy approached me and gave me a big hug. Neither of them had any idea what they witnessed, but they knew I was a changed man. God had not only given His Son to die on the cross for me, but He also took me in His arms and freed me from the grip hatred had on my life.

Sandy put her arm around my waist, and we made our way up and out of the maze. Outside, we spotted Val and Juli in the field some distance away. We waved our hands in their direction, and they came running up to meet us.

While we waited for them to join us, I reached over to Phil and gave him a big hug and told him I loved him. I said the same to Juli and then to Val when they got there. I wanted them to know how appreciative I was for their support. I wanted them to know how much I loved them. I would do anything for my family.

"Thank you for being here with me. Thank you for trying to understand and love me through all of this," I said.

I could see Val shoot Sandy a questioning look. I'm sure she wondered what had happened while we were in there. I would tell her later, but first I wanted to see if I could get those records. After all, we *had* come all this way.

I continued to hum that praise song as we walked up to the commandants' headquarters. I held Val's hand the entire way. Life was going to be okay. No matter what I found, I knew who I was and I knew I was loved. I may have been rejected by people my entire life, but God had never once rejected me. He understood me. He knew my highs and my lows, and He still accepted me. Though my quest for the pieces of my past was not nearly over, I had peace knowing that God would be by my side every step of the way. And at the end of the day — and ultimately, at the end of my life — that's all that matters.

Afterword

After his visit to Stutthof Concentration Camp, Peter returned to the United States a changed man. The hatred he felt toward all those who had wronged him began to slowly melt away with the help and guidance of God.

Today, Peter travels around the United States, Europe, and Israel ministering to those who seek healing through forgiveness. Millions of people have suffered tragedies in their lives, but few have been able to truly forgive those who have wronged them. Through his remarkable testimony, God has given Peter the experiential voice and compassion needed to reach those who have suffered greatly from their pasts.

Jobst Bittner is a German pastor who initiated the "March of Life," an event that followed the tracks of the death marches from the Swabian Alb to Dachau and caused healing and reconciliation for both Germans and Jews. Here he shares his first experience with Peter's testimony:

Our city of Tübingen, Germany, is a university town with long-standing traditions and great influence, similar to Harvard or Oxford. But Tübingen has a dismal past. The very foundation of the university was based on anti-Semitism and the expulsion of the Jews. At the time of the Nazi regime, the university was the first in Germany "free of Jews." The city's synagogue was burned to the ground, and one of the mayors was responsible for the murder of thousands of people in a mass shooting on the Balkan. So when Peter Loth spoke at our church in Tübingen, we were stunned.

"Can you forgive me?" he asked.

Standing before us was a Holocaust survivor. Since the moment of his birth he had been tormented and maltreated — deserted by his mother, tortured as a boy, imprisoned, at all times just a step away from death. And now here we were, descendants of the S.S. officers, soldiers or even just the silent majority who watched millions of Jews be deported and murdered in the concentration camps. Why on earth should he return to Germany, the land he would have every right to hate most? Why was he asking our forgiveness?

I will never forget that first meeting with Peter. He presented moving and shocking pictures from his time in the concentration camp. At times, he too had to struggle with tears, and yet he kept repeating, "This is healing, even though it causes infinite pain every time I speak about my life!"

"I used to hate you Germans," Peter said. And again he asked that question, "Can you forgive me?" There were many thoughts that raced through my mind. I struggled for words as I tried to voice the most pressing among them. So I got up, declared forgiveness, and then said to him, "Here are the descendants of those who have destroyed your life. Many of them are descendants of S.S. officers, war criminals or anti-Semites. Most of them have never asked for forgiveness! We need your forgiveness. Can we ask you for forgiveness?"

Peter opened his arms and answered, "Come, I want to hug you and proclaim forgiveness for each and every one of you." What happened next was more than I could ever have imagined. God visited the tent with His mercy and grace. His glory was all over. There were lines of people, waiting patiently to be hugged and embraced. They were weighed down by the burden of their forefathers, but they had never confessed their guilt. Here was a Jewish father, willing to take them into his arms and to break the chains over them through his love.

It was a dramatic sight. Many broke down weeping, others fell to the ground under the power of God and received healing. Peter stood there for several hours to embrace every single one waiting in the line and to proclaim forgiveness and release. I watched the faces of those leaving that holy place. They were radiant with joy and peace, because they had encountered the reconciling grace of Yeshua. Weeks later, I still heard testimonies of deliverance from bitterness and of reconciliation.

All who have heard Peter Loth's life story will have to face one question: What right do I have to hold on to bitterness or to hold any man's sin against him? Our answer to this question will determine our future. Bitterness and unforgiveness quench all life. The Bible says that unforgiveness makes us prisoners and keeps us from knowing the freedom of the children of God. Peter left behind his last prison forever. His life story is a message to us all. Forgiveness is the open door for change and life.

If you, your church, or your organization is interested in hearing Peter Loth's testimony firsthand, please visit the Forerunner Ministries International, Inc. website at www. forerunnerministries.org for a schedule of speaking events.

LaVergne, TN USA
21 October 2010
201687LV00004B/2/P